HEINRICH DUMOULIN has lived in Japan since 1935 and is Professor of Philosophy and History of Religion at Sophia University in Tokyo. He is a correspondent counsellor to the Vatican Committee for the Dialogue with Non-Christian Religions and the author of *A History of Zen Buddhism* and editor of

ıth standard

philosophy

Rahner and

laude from the University of Munich in 1970 for his work in hermeneutics. A former Kent Fellow, he has served as Assistant Professor of Philosophy at Loyola University, Los Angeles, and at Sophia University, Tokyo, where he is presently engaged in research into Oriental thought.

Christianity Meets Buddhism

Religious Encounter: East and West

Christianity Meets Buddhism
   by Heinrich Dumoulin

Zen Meditation and Christian Mysticism
   by H. M. Enomiya Lassalle

Christianity Meets Buddhism

Heinrich Dumoulin
Translated by John C. Maraldo

1974
Open Court Publishing Company
LaSalle, Illinois

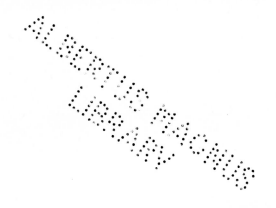

Printed in the United States of America

Library of Congress Catalogue Card Number: 73-82783
ISBN: 0-87548-121-3

Religious Encounter: East and West

"Religious Encounter: East and West" is a series of books intended to promote an understanding of the living unity, diversity and meeting-ground of religious phenomena, Asian and Occidental. Published under the auspices of the Institute for the Study of Oriental Religions of Sophia University, Tokyo, the series strives to apply modern methods of scholarship to some questions of perennial and present relevance, and to employ some recent experiences in order to enrich and nourish communication among mankind. This endeavor continues the special mission of Sophia University, founded by an international group of Jesuits some 60 years ago, and serves as a platform of intercultural exchange and interreligious encounter.

The publications of this series treat the great religions of the two hemispheres from varying points of view, considering the entirety and the constituents of one religion in relation to another. This spectrum of viewpoints has perhaps only recently been made possible by the fulfillment of certain historical conditions which allow freer religious intercourse. Thus the historical situation itself constitutes a part of the matter under reflection in the series. The fact that religions too are subject to the penetrating social changes of our day must be accounted for. The widely observed process of secularization which is exerting a powerful influence on the course of human religious practice should not be taken for granted. On the one hand, it has facilitated an extraordinary increase in the extent and the intensity of religious dialogue during the last few decades. On the other, the ensuing pace of cultural evolution restricts any prognosis of ready achievements within the sphere of dialogue.

Under these conditions, the range of both the topics and the contributors of "Religious Encounter: East and West" has intentionally been kept as wide as the thematic permits. It is thereby hoped that the Eastern and Western authors, belonging to various religions, can present the reader with food for thought sufficient to open him to new perspectives. The series operates on the principle that the open and free exchange of ideas is both a goal worthy in itself and a foundation of constructive development of the great cultural traditions in East and West.

Heinrich Dumoulin, Editor
John C. Maraldo, Associate Editor

CONTENTS

Christianity Meets Buddhism

PROLOGUE

For the first time in history, Buddhism and Christianity are openly and intentionally encountering each other today, and in many lands. This encounter comes in a time of change and even crisis. Technology is forcing man to envision a new world unity, and at the same time threatening to manipulate nature and man so as to give man the technologist control over mankind's welfare —or mankind's destruction.

What role can the religions play in this age? Are they destined to decline, to be crushed from without, emptied from within, to vanish from the face of the earth? Buddhism and Christianity both face new and unusual—perhaps unprecedented—tasks.

We cannot foresee how these two religions will stand in face of that crisis. It is possible that some things which this book says will be obsolete in a few years' time. Nevertheless it is worth our while to examine the encounter between Buddhism and Christianity to see what we can learn from that encounter in this time of crisis. This book approaches that theme from various sides: it reports interreligious conferences and personal contacts, considers the influences of the times on the East-West encounter, reflects on the significance of spiritual and mystical experiences, and takes up both theological and metaphysical perspectives. Much of what it says comes from conversations; some of its viewpoints arose from a closer study of themes inspired by the discussions. Almost all the important aspects of the Buddhist-Christian encounter are at least touched upon, though it has proved impossible to develop the full extent and meaning of every pertinent question, especially those of a strictly philosophical nature. This book attempts to see Buddhism and Christianity together as religions and for this purpose, tries to clarify wide areas of religious teaching and religious practice as they bear upon the modern dialogue.

The relation between Buddhism and Christianity is regarded here in the light of their encounter and their dialogue, seeking to deepen mutual understanding. This dialogue has been carried on in openness and respect, and has created an atmosphere of mutual interest and growth. And since the plurality of religions is assumed as a fact, committed Buddhists and committed Christians can meet together in dialogue as equitable partners, and seek to understand and to learn from each other.

Participants in the interreligious dialogue esteem "what human beings have in common and what promotes fellowship among them." The Second Vatican Council, which characterized the attitude of dialogue with these words, set down in its documents several important points for the Christian partner who seeks to value the religious traditions of mankind and to appreciate the non-Christian religions. In its "Dogmatic Constitution on the Church," the Council recognized the possibility of attaining salvation outside of the institutional Church and without an explicit belief in Christ (No. 16), and thus removed a longstanding barrier to interreligious relations. And the Council's "Declaration on the Relationship of the Church to Non-Christian Religions," recounts specific religious values of some of the great religions. Through his belief in the guidance of God, whose "saving designs extend to all men" (No. 1), the Christian can recognize God's saving action at work in all religions. He can, if he turns to others with an open heart and mind, grow to see that the Far Eastern religions which disclose precious values of inner life, could not have emerged without some kind of divine assistance. Although this book does not extensively treat the new "theology of religons" in this respect, it proceeds from the conviction that the non-Christian religions contribute to the salvation of mankind, and that recognition of this may pave the way for fruitful discussion.

In the dialogue with Buddhism, Christianity presents itself as a complex religion not easily comprehended. Likewise, for Christians, the phenomenon of Buddhism is ramified and difficult to grasp. The Westerner often finds himself of two minds about Asia and Asian culture: he experiences a strong leaning, and at the same time an inner resistance toward Eastern matters. Far Eastern spirituality enchants him, but appears enigmatic in many respects. The religion of the Buddha

seems particularly paradoxical, not so much with regard to its complicated doctrines as to the many faces
of its living practice. Western authors have frequently
simplified the issues by presenting only a part of Buddhism for the whole, in pursuit of a consistent system
of their own making. This book deliberately refrains
from this kind of systematizing. It instead considers the
various branches of Buddhism, and lets oppositions and
even contradictions stand as they are, in order to do as
much justice as possible to the immense complexity of
the subject. One need not immediately infer that the
principle of contradiction does not hold true for Asians;
in the realm of religious experience and faith, however,
things at first sight opposed often exist side by side.

We must also consider how the two great world religions of East and West are part of the process of world
history. We know that religions as humans paths to
salvation, in spite of their inherent and everlasting principles, change over the centuries, integrating new elements and adapting their changing forms to the needs
of the times. Change is especially evident today. Christianity has awakened the interest of a wide public in our
day, in part because of its desire to adapt to modern
times. The modifications Buddhism is undergoing are
hardly less intense, and are strikingly similar to movements in the Western world. Thus the two religions
meet today, while striving to renew themselves. The
encounter is by nature complex, and its relevance has
not yet been adequately probed.

This book has no certain conclusions to present.
Rather, it considers aspects which seek to clarify, and
to inspire, further clarification of the many questions
involved in the Buddhist-Christian dialogue. It hopes
to draw attention to and awaken understanding of the
encounter between Buddhism and Christianity. The

success of this dialogue, like the expansion of fellowship among men on earth, is contingent upon the change Arnold Toynbee spoke of when he wrote, "The change of the heart is the heart of the matter" (*Experience,* Oxford University Press, 1969, p. 329).

Some of the material of the first two chapters of this book was formerly published in the German study, *Christlicher Dialog mit Asien* (Max Hueber Verlag, Munich, 1970). I wish to thank Iwao Hoshii for rendering these chapters into English. I am deeply grateful to John C. Maraldo for his efforts in translating and editing the final English version of the book. The publishers have my heartfelt thanks for their undertaking of this project, the first in the series "Religious Encounter: East and West."

H. D.

CHAPTER I

Preparing the Occident for the Dialogue with the Orient

Today the outline of a universal human culture is clearly discernible. And it is the task of our times to lay the foundations, personal and institutional, for this culture. Particularly important is the encounter of the Occident with Asia. These two highly advanced cultures, which developed largely independently over thousands of years, are now moving closer to each other on a broad front. The dialogue between East and West counts as one of the decisive events of our era. Technological progress has created the possibility for all peoples and races to communicate with one another, by overcoming the obstacle of distance and by providing the material requisites for a uniform civilization embracing the entire world. Of the many themes of this dialogue, that of religion, because of its dignity and its importance, deserves priority. It is for this reason that we approach the problems of the basic dialogue with Asia from the point of view of religion.

The study of the Far Eastern religions and cultures provides the basis for a wide and deep cultural exchange between East and West. This exchange is greatly facilitated by the technological achievements bringing people into the closest contact with one another. But we know that technological progress alone will be unable to effect a true union of mankind, if there does not arise a new spirit of universal brotherhood.

Pope John XXIII, with his penetrating intuitive vision, recognized the misery and true anguish of mankind, and by his own life demonstrated convincingly the virtue of brotherhood. He cordially received people of all faiths and all races, and his goodness left an unforgettable impression on them. The Pope spoke to non-Christians of the common ground of faith of all religious men, and expressed his conviction that all men of good will should cooperate for the welfare of all mankind.

In a similar way, Pope Paul VI, prior to his historic journey to India in December 1964, declared that "It is absolutely necessary that we have a much more outspoken desire for human brotherhood." In order to promote and deepen the contacts with non-Christian religions, Pope Paul established a secretariat in Rome under the direction of Cardinal Marella. In March 1965, when Cardinal Marella came to Japan, and again on the occasion of his visit to the World's Fair in Osaka in the summer of 1970, he met with many representatives of non-Christian religions in Tokyo, Kyoto and Hiroshima. It was astonishing with what sincere joy these leading Buddhists, Shintoists and other non-Christians received the Cardinal. In his first address, he assured them that "Mutual understanding, brotherliness and cordiality must replace distrust and threats. How could we better achieve this than through the harmony and the mutual support of religions, which aim at leading men through their hearts to the meaning of obligation and charity?" Just as in India Pope Paul quoted from the Upanishads, so Cardinal Marella cited in Japan a saying of the Buddhist Emperor Asoka, dating from the third century B.C., which had recently been discovered in an inscription in Central Asia. "The victory I consider the greatest is the victory of compassion."

If we are pleased with the technological achievements of our century, we must, at the same time, be aware that only the spirit of brotherhood, of mutual understanding and love, can bring real progress and assure the true happiness of mankind. Only in this spirit can an encounter between East and West be successful and a true unity between these two hemispheres be effected.

The differences and contrasts are of course enormous. "East is East, and West is West, and never the twain shall meet," as it is said in Kipling's often quoted verse. We cannot overlook or minimize those differences. Is it not exactly these differences which founded two great world cultures in independence of each other? The technology of the West has brought the countries of Asia under its dominion, and to a large extent, has conquered the material world. The spiritual chasm between the continents cannot be spanned by material means. Yet there is a complementary relationship between the two.

The Complementary Relationship Between Far Eastern and Western Thinking

Basically, all Far Eastern cultures are religious. Even in this era of increasing secularization, the Eastern mind retains its essentially religious outlook. True, many institutions and organizations in the Eastern countries are falling into decay, particularly in Japan where modernization has made the most progress. Nevertheless, religious forces remain active. The influence of tradition in Japan has not inappropriately been compared to the workings of the collective unconscious. Carl Jung pointed out the remarkable parallel "between the unconscious psyche of the West and the 'manifest' psyche of the East." In his opinion, "the spirit of the Far East stands in the same relation to the consciousness of the West as the unconscious to the conscious, or the left hand to the right."[1] These words are interesting in many respects, not least because of the obvious conclusion to be drawn from them that neither the Eastern nor Western mind alone and unaided can encompass the totality of the human spirit; neither represents the totality of human culture. The Eastern mind and the Western mind are complementary to each other. Human culture can only be brought to perfection in an exchange between the two hemispheres, and this requires mutual understanding and genuine cooperation.

In the course of this century, the Far Eastern religions have attracted considerable interest in the Western world. In some European countries and in the United States, something like a boom in Oriental religions developed, a pursuit of Asian religiosity comparable to the flowering of Oriental cults in imperial Rome. But whoever is engaged more than superficially in things Oriental, who perseveres in their serious pursuit, will leave the ephemeral and faddish far behind.

Curiously enough, religious forms quite alien to the West (such as Yoga and Zen Buddhism) have excited the most interest, while religious attitudes more akin to Christianity (such as India's theistically oriented *bhakti* devotion, or the veneration of the Buddha Amida in Japan) attracted less attention. One reason for this may be the complementarity between Eastern and Western thinking suggested by Jung. Western man, particularly the modern Westerner, is inclined to become completely engrossed in external pursuits. Psychologically speaking, he is an extrovert, whereas Eastern man is the introvert capable of intense experiences of himself as well as of nature. This capacity seems to have survived even in Japan's modern cities and has relieved the strains of mass society. The tension between the inward and outward tendencies in man constitutes a fundamental factor of human existence and plays an important role in today's encounter between East and West. The Eastern mind can impart to the West its contemplative heritage, and the West, too, is called upon to communicate. A genuine exchange from both sides is required if the encounter of East and West is to bring forth its fruit for mankind.

It is because of the peculiarity of today's situation that the specific values of Far Eastern mentality are understood and accepted in the West as never before. On the one hand, it is acutely felt that these values promise to fill up some serious deficiencies of Western man. On the other hand, the new Christian theology of the Second Vatican Council, perhaps coincidentally, rediscovered basic values and attitudes which had been lost for centuries in the West, but were traditionally rooted and highly developed in Asia. The discussion following will examine some of these specifically Eastern values in their relevance to today's spiritual situation in the Occident.

Stillness and Meditation

Most evident is the attitude of Far Eastern meditation which can be regarded as the prerequisite of all higher spiritual life. According to an old Sino-Japanese saying, "Stillness lies in motion and motion in stillness." Stillness and motion are the two poles of all activities of human life. Neither of the two poles should be neglected. Only if stillness and motion are coordinated, can man attain his complete consummation in the equilibrium of his powers.

In Asia, meditation serves principally to integrate the self. It is the "Great Path" to which the other little paths of the arts and sciences are subordinate. Meditation is performed in silence and leads man into ever deeper regions of silence until that silence is reached for which there is no word, of which the Buddha said, "I have heard silence." At the same time, however, meditation releases man's inner energies. In several forms of Eastern meditation, in the *kōan* practice of Zen Buddhism, for example[2], the exertion is quite manifest; but even the mere sitting posture of meditation is animated from within, and the disciple remains constantly and completely awake. While he endeavors to empty his mind of all stirrings of the imagination, of all discursive thinking and conceptual ideas, the stillness in him becomes more still. This stillness does not come easily. Rather, if it blooms in the innermost self, it is the fruit of a long nurturing. Stillness and motion are simultaneously present during the entire exercise.

Modern Western man, rushing from achievement to achievement, has to a large degree lost the harmony of his self and the inner balance of stillness and motion. Too often the two poles of human activity are disrupted in him. He feels a nostalgic longing for the lost paradise of stillness. Le Corbusier understood his artistic work in relation to the plight of modern man, and in his life wrote with gratitude, "I have worked for what today's man needs most, stillness and peace." In his distress, modern Western man turns readily to Eastern ways of meditation which seem to possess a special timeliness, because in them the two poles of stillness and motion are admirably brought together.[3] It can only be a gain for the Occident if the attempt at a spiritual encounter with Asia proceeds from the Far Eastern ways of meditation.

Exterior and Interior, Body and Soul

Like the rhythm of breathing, stillness and motion flow from the polar activity of human life.[4] Equally fundamental to man's existence is the polar coordination and interdependence of exterior and interior, body and soul. The harmony of the human personality rests on the accord of internal and external faculties, the oneness of the spiritual and corporeal, of soul and body. The belief that man forms a whole, in the unity of spirit and flesh, is particularly awake in the Far East. The peculiarity of Eastern meditation springs from this conviction. As understood and practiced by the peoples of the Far East, meditation is not exclusively a mental and inner activity, but is accomplished in unison with the body. Body and soul cooperate. Eastern man has an experiential awareness of the psychic and somatic aspects of human actions. Asians are not materialists. The spirit is the leader, but human existence is one, corporeal as well as spiritual.

In Zen Buddhism, meditating while sitting in the posture of the lotus seat (*padmāsana*), the so-called *zazen*, is a physical and psychic exercise; it is considered an almost indispensable prerequisite for obtaining enlightenment. The Japanese Zen masters express the unity of spirit and body in Zen exercises by the word *sugata*, meaning figure or shape; it indicates the wholeness of the psychosomatic "gestalt" of the disciple sitting in meditation. According to a saying of the famous 13th century Zen master, Dōgen, the figure of the disciple seated in meditation expresses the enlightenment of the Buddha.[5]

In its encounter with Asia, the Occident can renew the conviction also present in Western tradition that the unity of body and soul comprises the fundamental wholeness of man. This conviction forms part of man's basic knowledge about his mode of existence. Under the predominant influence of Greek philosophy, the Occident has, if not entirely forgotten, at least for centuries not sufficiently experienced this unity. The dualistic attitude toward reality, propounded in an extreme form by Plato (*sōma-sēma* theory) and upheld in a mitigated version by Aristotle (*anima forma corporis*), has widely influenced Western culture. Platonic and gnostic dualism has penetrated into Christian doctrine and even more deeply into Christian life, asceticism and spirituality. Today, it is generally recognized that the original Christian understanding of man contained in the Bible differs from the dualistic Greek view. According to the Old and New Testaments, as well as to Semitic tradition, man is a whole: the spirit is man and the body is man. It is inexact and incomplete, therefore, to say that man has a body. The truth is: man is body and man is spirit.[6]

In the Middle Ages, the Jewish religion as well as Christianity might have lost entirely the conviction of man's basic unity, had it not been for their belief in the resurrection of the flesh. In Christian doctrine, this belief is linked with the belief in the Resurrection of Christ and the Incarnation of the Logos. The belief in the Resurrection is a belief in the perfect integration of man in the oneness of spirit and body. The human body will be transfigured by the *pneuma,* the Spirit, in imitation of the perfect man, Christ.

Unfortunately, the biblical conception of the fundamental unity of man has not shaped the Occidental tradition in the way it should have. Since early times, Christian theology has been strongly influenced by a Neoplatonism which overemphasized the dualistic aspect of human existence, the tension between spirit and flesh. This tension also belongs to man's fundamental experiences and is felt with particular poignancy by sinful man. Nevertheless, Christian anthropology, for example the anthropology of Thomas Aquinas, cannot simply be labeled dualistic, even though it interprets the teaching of the Bible with the help of the categories of Aristotelian philosophy.[7] Today we are experiencing the return of modern Catholic theology to the pure sources of revelation, above all Holy Scripture. We may hope that this theology, which is guided by the biblical view of man in his oneness, created in God's likeness as spirit and body, as man and woman, will overcome the Greek dualism. The distinctive feature of the Christian conception of man and attitude toward life is not the dualistic component stressed by the consciousness of sin, but rather the belief that man was created in God's image and likeness.

The recovery of the biblical view of man prepares the Occident for the dialogue with Asia. Taught by the Bible, the faithful Christian may gain a better and deeper understanding of Far Eastern spirituality, while the contact with Far Eastern meditation can help him toward a fuller realization of biblical truth. The new attitude toward the body neither overestimates corporeal powers and the beauty of the body in a materialistic fashion, nor despises or neglects the body after the manner of Neoplatonism or gnosticism. It is thoroughly biblical and can, at the same time, be regarded as a precious treasure of Asian spirituality. According to this view, the spirit finds its most perfect expression in the body through meditation, while the body is integrated progressively into the total, clear and wakeful consciousness of the spirit.

Intuitive Knowledge

With an integral view of man, Asia combines the integral thinking of intuitive knowledge. Here again are important points of contact for the dialogue.

It is known that the ways of thinking of Eastern and Western peoples are appreciably different from each other. To be sure, it is only with certain reservations that we can speak of a typically Asiatic way of thinking. Those who have traveled through the countries of Asia have been impressed by the wide variety of the numerous cultures of the Asian peoples. Nevertheless, there is a kind of basic unity which allows us to speak not only of an Asian continent but also of a typically Asian way of thinking. We might probe this mode of thinking best if we search among the manifold appearances of

Far Eastern spirituality for that intuitive power which the Eastern mind turns toward the concrete aspects of reality.

In Asia, the ways of intuitive knowledge are linked to the ways of meditation. Man's encounter with reality through meditation is effectively expressed in a phrase often used by the Japanese Zen masters: *koto ni fureru* (literally, "to touch things"). It is intended to convey that man, in his knowledge, makes contact with concrete, real things as they are, that he must hit upon them in their center (the Japanese would say in their *hara,* their belly).[8] And, conversely, it is the innermost nucleus of the human person which must touch the reality of things. A man who touches things in this way will invariably respond to all the stimuli of reality.

In contrast, Occidental thinking has developed an undeniable preference for abstract concepts. It is certainly true that, through abstract analytical and methodical thinking, Western science has created the dominant world civilization. Nevertheless, the abstract scientific way of thinking is limited and one-sided. This other way of thinking, intuitive knowledge, must be included if human culture is to develop fully.

Naturally the Occidental tradition also embodies its own various forms of intuitive knowledge and symbolic expression, analogous to what has been called Eastern integral thinking. A strong current of Platonism, extolling man's intuitive powers, runs through Occidental philosophy. Above all I would draw attention to the treasure of integral thinking given in Holy Scripture to the Christian peoples of Europe. The Word that God spoke to mankind has not been handed down to us in abstract terms and conceptual definitions, but in concrete speech, close to palpable reality and rich in symbols and figures, parables and similies. Man is invited to listen to God's Word not only with his reason, but with his entire person.

Earlier generations of theologians have often felt, it seems, a kind of intellectual discomfort with the preponderantly figurative manner of speech of the Bible. Why did God prefer to speak to mankind mainly in parables? Why did he not use conceptual language, abstract terms and definitions? Abstract concepts, they thought, would have been much clearer and less equivocal than the concrete language of the Bible.

This way of thinking stems from a fatal error concerning human understanding. It overlooks the essential limitation of abstract thinking and conceptual language. Abstract thinking can neither comprehend the whole of reality nor can conceptual language express it. The reality of being exists beyond all concepts and words.

This underlies the Eastern way of thinking in negations, the preference of Asia's great sages for the negative way of approaching reality by saying what it is not. In reply to the question about the essence of the Supreme Being, Brahman, a wise teacher of the Upanishads said *"neti neti"*—"it is not so and it is not so." At about the same time, approximately 500 years before Christ, Lao-tzu in China described the "Tao" entirely by negations. Theravāda Buddhism calls the final state of deliverance, sought as the end of man's pilgrimage, Nirvāna. In Mahāyāna Buddhism, Nāgārjuna became the great master of the negative theology which later inspired the paradoxical *kōan* problems in Zen Buddhism. The negative way of the Far Eastern religions should not be misinterpreted as nihilism. In thought as well as meditation, the significance of the negative way consists in inducing man to break through the categories of logical thinking and to attain superrational en-

lightment. At the root of this lies the conviction that
the highest intuitive knowledge, which Eastern man
hopes to attain through meditation, cannot be expressed
in human words and concepts.[9]

Less noticed than the Eastern preference for the
negative way of thinking is the fact that Christian revelation, as taught through Holy Scripture, also possesses
a negative theology. God is the ineffable mystery. The
mystery of God which constitutes the central core of
divine revelation also cannot be expressed adequately
by human words and concepts.[10]

This is true not only for the mystery of God's inner
life, of the Blessed Trinity, but also for the infinite reality of God the Creator. The metaphorical language of
the Bible, its wealth of symbols and similies, has been
inspired by the unutterable mystery of God. The Word
of God, infinitely higher than all words of man, finds
its purest and truest expression not in the precise formulations of scientific theology, not in the categorical definitions of the councils, but in the necessarily veiled
images of Holy Scripture.

Today many competent observers see clearly that
mysticism is called upon to play an important role in
the encounter with Asiatic religions. The dialogue with
the East impels Christianity to harken back to its own
mystical tradition, while Buddhists can learn to evaluate their own spiritual masters on the basis of their true
value. The authentic mystical experiences in East and
West converge, and the points of contact are not limited
to the highest forms. The entire way of higher meditation in Christianity and Zen Buddhism glows with the
fervor of mysticism.

In the history of thought, the turn of modern theology to the sources is of epochal significance. In this
hour when the Occident meets Asia, the Spirit of God

leads theology in a direction in which it can meet
Asian thinking. The gracious guidance of God is discernible in the preparatory work modern theology
has done for the dialogue with Asia. Through its new
approach to Scripture, and its deeper understanding
of the Word of God, today's Christian theology has
gained access to the soul of the peoples of the Far
East.

The Threat to Mankind's Spiritual Culture

What has been said above has indicated a few of the
most significant values which are needed by Western
man and for which Western thinking is preparing itself.
Stillness and meditation, oneness of spirit and body,
intuitive awareness of the truth touching the mystery
of reality—all these lie deeply within man, at the very
root of his existence. They are by no means the exclusive
possession of Far Eastern spirituality, but are embedded
(if forgotten) in Western tradition. We here touch common ground.

Yet these same basic values, the foundation of all
higher spiritual culture, are threatened today by a technological world culture promoting a materialistic attitude and evading the claims of the spiritual. In Asia as
well as in the Occident, spiritual treasures are being
squandered. This materialism poses grave problems to
the whole of mankind, and only united action can solve
them.

The threat to spiritual values developed with the
rapid progress of the natural sciences. The tremendous
influence of today's science is felt equally in Asia and

in the Western countries. But the reaction to the impact is not necessarily the same in the two hemispheres. From time immemorial, Eastern man has been living in close proximity to nature. Rather than feeling himself surrounded by nature, he feels himself embedded and implanted in it. He experiences within himself the all-embracing symmetry of the two central cosmic realities, the microcosm of his self and the macrocosm of the universe. Like his Western brother, Eastern man is aware of his responsibility for the world, though his awareness is of a different sort. How can he tame the powers of the universe, how can he utilize the forces of nature? For centuries introversion led him to attempt the conquest of nature through the powers of meditation; he was convinced that whoever could become master of the powers of the microcosm of his own self, would also be able to master the macrocosm, the entire universe. This conviction of the omnipotence of the spiritual, impressive though it may be, failed to find credence with Western man. Nor should it be forgotten that today Eastern man too is no longer satisfied with it. At an early date, Western man turned his attention to the outside, explored the world surrounding him, detected the laws governing the cosmic forces, and succeeded in utilizing them. Through this awe-inspiring triumph of methodical research, man conquered nature. Whatever this may connote to us, the fact remains that in this age of technological achievement the natural sciences have created a new world.

Is this world devoid of spirituality? Does a technological civilization necessarily degenerate into materialism? Is there any connection between the cosmos of modern science and the highly spiritualized cosmos of the Far Eastern cultures? These questions touch the core of modern man's basic problem. So far, they have not found a satisfactory answer.

The World-View of Teilhard de Chardin and Far Eastern Spirituality

Searching for a view which maintains the balance of a scientific world culture and an interior spiritual life, without attributing to either of them an absolute value, we come to the works of Teilhard de Chardin. Under the conditions of the modern world, he shows us the way to a new reconciliation of interior and exterior, stillness and motion—or to use a pair of concepts familiar in the Occidental tradition, *vita contemplativa* and *vita activa.*[11] His world-view can serve as an example of how a future exchange between West and East might be implemented.

Teilhard's greatest achievement may have been his ability to awaken new confidence in the possibility of a true spirituality for a modern man committed to scientific thinking, despite growing skepticism and the general spiritual uncertainty of our age. His thoughts may need further theological and philosophical elaboration, but as a philosopher and a scientist, even more as a spiritual man and a European Christian who spent many years in Asia, Teilhard made a profound contribution to our dialogue.

Teilhard wrote on 7 August 1923, in a letter to his friend Leontine Zanta, that he "had gone to China in hopes of finding a reservoir of thought and mysticism which could renew the life of the West." From the very first days of his sojourn in China, he had had "the impression that the reservoir was empty (or at least clogged up)." Nevertheless, the spiritual relationship of East and West was his lifelong concern. He intended "to write something novel about the basic question of metaphysics and religion: 'What is the manifold, and how can one unify it?' " (letter to L. Zanta, 20 March 1932). In answer, putting the Western and Eastern solutions together seemed indispensable to him. In an unpublished writing. *"Comment je crois,"* Teilhard noted that he was particularly receptive to Eastern influences. At the same time, he realized he and the East understood the same words to mean different things. "The East fascinates me for its belief in an ultimate unity of the universe. But it happens that it and I have quite contrary ideas about the mutual relationship between the whole and its parts. For the East, unity arises from suppression; for me it grows from concentration."[12] Thus Teilhard saw the Eastern striving for unity in direct contrast to that of the West—the West is oriented toward tension and concentration, the East toward release and dissolution.

Even in his later years, when he was animated with the idea of a new universal and spiritualized world culture, he approached the problem as a Westerner. He consciously avoided propounding a new world-view as a *synthesis* of Eastern and Western elements; instead he was convinced that a solution had to come from the West, although not without the contribution of the East. Proceeding "on the Western road," he thought mankind would arrive at a new universal world-view embracing the East and West. Through the gate opened by the Western mind, all currents of human culture, its Eastern as well as its Western streams, would flow into the universal spiritual culture of mankind.

In a later article entitled *"L'Apport spirituel de l'Extrême Orient,"*[13] Teilhard set forth his view on Asia's contribution to the formation of the new world. He asserted that Far Eastern spirituality would fulfill "an indispensable role and an essential function" in the formative process; it could strengthen and enrich the new human and Christian mysticism." As noted above, Teilhard envisioned the new world culture in "its ascent from the West." In his all-embracing concept of evolution, the universe moves through the stages of cosmogenesis, bio-genesis and noo-genesis toward its goal, the highest spiritual and personal reality, Christ. This Christian interpretation of the deepest meaning of the modern knowledge of nature is not merely Western in its view, but claims universal validity.

Despite Teilhard's own assessment of his path as a Western one, his world-view is strikingly similar to Far Eastern ways of thinking. His convictions, perhaps more than he himself was aware of, involved a mutual interaction of Eastern and Western approaches. The feeling of cosmic interdependence, so characteristic of the religious experience of Asia, was one of the impelling forces of Teilhard's thinking. He sensed in a truly Eastern way the universal interaction of reality. "All things are linked with all things." His writings bring to mind one of the central themes of the religious literature of Asia, the law of karma which encompasses all physical and moral reality.

"Where are the roots of our being?" asks Teilhard in *Le Milieu Divin.*

". . . They plunge back and down into the unfathomable past . . . How impossible to decipher the synthesis of successive influences in which we are for ever incorporated! In each one of us, through matter, the whole history of the world is in part reflected. And however autonomous our soul, it is heir to an existence worked upon from all sides—before ever it came into being—by the totality of the energies of the earth . . . Let us look around us: the waves come from all sides and from the farthest horizon. Through every cleft the sensible world inundates us with its riches—food for the body, nourishment for the eyes, harmony of sounds and fullness for the heart, unknown phenomena and new truths . . . They will merge into the most intimate life of our soul, and either develop it or poison it. We only have to look at ourselves for one moment to realize this, and feel either delight or anxiety . . . We have not, in us, a body to be nourished independently of our soul. Everything that the body has admitted and has begun to transform must be sublimated by the soul in its turn . . . it cannot escape from this universal contact nor from that unremitting labor. . . . In each soul, God loves and partly saves the whole world which that soul sums up in an incommunicable and particular way . . ."[14]

Through an immense spiritual effort, Teilhard was able to recognize in outline the oneness and solidarity of the universe. He lived in the realm of man, but he grasped the realm of God because he fully understood that all reality is divine and demands from man a religious response. The divine does not exist outside the realm of man but is present everywhere, and man, endowed with the sense of the holy, can see the divine light shining through all existing things. Teilhard calls this capability with which man senses the divine presence, "the taste for being" (*le goût de l'être*).

This taste for being is a natural faculty of the soul. Man can be misled by this faculty and fall prey to one of the many forms of pantheism, and Teilhard warns clearly and explicitly against such deviations. In his view, the taste for being is a precious gift of God which enables man to perceive the divine presence in all things. To awaken this taste for being in modern man is a task which all education and personal guidance should undertake. If this can be done, world civilization will present no serious threat to the spiritual culture of man.

The encounter of East and West must of course engage all mankind, but in a particular way it is a task for Western Christianity. There is, moreover, a relation between the tendency toward modernization observable in today's Japanese Buddhism[15] and some of the new approaches in Christian theology. The demythologizing reappraisal of tradition is a common trait of all religions in the 20th century. Considerably more important are the anthropological tenets of the new Christian theology; these facilitate the building of bridges to human values in non-Christian religions. Hereafter, the new insights gained through theological renewal will exercise a stronger influence on the interreligious dialogue, to the extent in which they will be able to combine universality with a genuine pluralism of thought and sentiment. The motives which in today's technological age provide the impetus to a dialogue between the religions can make it easier for man to find the correct point of departure and the attitude required for interreligious communication. The feeling of human solidarity awakened everywhere inspires the dialogue between the religions and will contribute to the formation of a suitable style.

Notes

1   Cf. Jung's Preface to L. Abegg, *Ostasien denkt anders* (Zurich, 1949), p. 4.

2   On Zen Buddhism, in addition to the works of D. T. Suzuki, see H. M. Enomiya-Lassalle, *Zen-Way to Enlightenment* (New York, 1968); Heinrich Dumoulin, *A History of Zen Buddhism*

(New York, 1963); Christmas Humphreys, *Zen Buddhism* (London, 1949), and *Zen: A Way of Life* (New York, 1965); Alan Watts, *The Way of Zen* (New York, 1957); Eugen Herrigel, *Zen in the Art of Archery* (New York, 1953).

3   See Karlfried Graf von Dürckheim, *Japan und die Kultur der Stille* (Munich, 1950); also the section entitled "Stille und Meditation" in Heinrich Dumoulin, *Östliche Meditation und christliche Mystik* (Freiburg and Munich, 1966), pp. 21-27.

4   Compare the idea of breathing in Goethe's poem, "Im Atemholen sind zweierlei Gnaden," *West-Östlicher Divan, Buch des Sängers,* ed. E. Bentler (Bremen, 1956), p. 7. In his *Dialogues,* Novalis as well speaks of a necessary "mixture of active strength and serene repose": Kluckholm-Samuel, vol. II (Stuttgart, 1965), p. 666f.

5   Dumoulin, *A History of Zen Buddhism,* pp. 159ff.

6   The holistic anthropological view that the spirit exists only in and as the body is supported by the new understanding of Scripture which is prevalent among today's theologians. Thus, Joseph Ratzinger writes that "Christian faith springs from the knowledge that man is most himself when he is braced by all: by mankind, by history, by the cosmos, and as a 'spirit in a body.' " *Einführung in das Christentum* (Munich, 1968), pp. 199f.

7   In a short treatise on the body, suffering and death, Ladislaus Boros, in *Erlöstes Dasein* (Mainz, 1965), pp. 31ff., points out that Thomas Aquinas, although he still used the concepts of body and soul, taught their inner unity in man and thus overcame the Greek dualism. Man, according to Aquinas, does not consist of "two different things," but rather is a unitary being in whom matter and spirit are essentially one. The human body, Boros continues, is the unfolding of the soul. And the human soul is the highest realization of matter; it unites with matter according to its nature. Without the body, there is no soul. Boros feels that Aquinas anticipated views that only hundreds of years later were even partially understood.

Today, when anthropology generally seeks to mend the dualistic separation, the notions "body" (*Leib*) and "being a body" (*Leibsein*) are often used to mean the whole man, the whole person and his being. M. Merleau-Ponty's notion of the *corps sujet,* for example, rejects a human existence of spiritless matter and immaterial spirit.

8   See Karlfried Graf von Dürckheim, *Hara, Die Erdmitte des Menschen* (3rd edition, Weilheim, 1967).

9   On negative theology in the Eastern tradition and in Christian mysticism, see Dumoulin, *Östliche Meditation und christliche Mystik,* pp. 104-124. The Japanese Christian philosopher M. Matsumoto once remarked in a lecture, "We have good reason to expect Mahāyāna Buddhism to offer a more enriched expression for the supernatural experience of God's omnipresence and especially of his transcendence."

10   The *theologia negativa* has received renewed attention in modern Catholic theology. It is already found in the Fathers of the Church; later it entered Scholastic theology through the Neoplatonic formulations of the Pseudo-Dionysius, and it is very conspicuous in medieval German mysticism. The speculative mysticism of Meister Eckhart attracted the attention of the Japanese philosophical school of Kitarō Nishida, which has been influenced by Zen Buddhism. In his reflections on the philosophy of religion, Keiji Nishitani, the present leader of the school, continually refers to Meister Eckhart. For a recent study on the parallels between Meister Eckhart and Zen Buddhism see S. Ueda, *Die Gottesgeburt in der Seele und der Durchbruch zur Gottheit,* subtitled "Die mystische Anthropologie Meister Eckharts und ihre Konfrontation mit der Mystik des Zen-Buddhismus" (Gütersloh, 1965). See also H. Waldenfels, "Absolute Nothingness: Preliminary Considerations on a Central Notion in the Philosophy of Nishida Kitaro and the Kyoto School," *Monumenta Nipponica,* vol. XXI (1966), pp. 354-391.

11   During its long history, the Occident has shown a remarkable fluctuation in evaluating the *vita contemplativa* and the *vita activa.* On the necessity of distinguishing the two and yet hold them in balance, see the philosophical study by Hannah Arendt, *The Human Condition* (Chicago, 1958).

12   Quoted by W. Kunz, "Das Denken des Fernen Ostens in der Sicht Teilhard de Chardins," *Perspektiven der Zukunft* (June 3, 1967), p. 6.

13   First published in Paris in the *Zeitschrift des jüdischen Denkens* (October 1950); later reprinted posthumously in *Monumenta Nipponica,* vol. XII (1956), pp. 1-11.

14   Pierre Teilhard de Chardin, *The Divine Milieu: An Essay on the Interior Life* (New York and Evanston, 1960), pp. 27-29.

15   Cf. Heinrich Dumoulin, "Der Buddhismus," *Die Erscheinungen und Kräfte der modernen Welt,* vol. II of *Weltgeschichte der Gegenwart,* (Bern and Munich, 1963), pp. 640ff.

CHAPTER 2

Buddhism and
Christianity in Dialogue

When we speak of the dialogue between Christianity and Buddhism, we refer not merely to a possibility but to something actually occurring.[1] We are dealing with meetings that have already taken place.

The meeting of Christianity and Buddhism is a recent occurrence; it is one of the innovations of the modern age and may rank among the most significant historical events of this era. Arnold Toynbee once concluded a lecture with the remark that a future historian, writing a thousand years hence about the 20th century, might take a greater interest in the first mutual penetration of Christianity and Buddhism than in the disagreements

between democratic and communist ideologies. We
may leave it to the future to judge the truth of Toynbee's speculation, but we may safely say in any case that
the dialogue between the two great world religions is
important.

As with all important events in the history of mankind, the dialogue between Buddhism and Christianity
did not originate accidentally. Nor was it pulled out of
thin air by a few idealistic nonconformists. Rather it
came into being exactly at the moment when the
spiritual situation of mankind was ripe for it. Even the
Second Vatican Council could only formulate its epochal "Declaration on the Relationship of the Church
to Non-Christian Religions" because the state of the
world required such guidance. And it is no accident that
the opening words of the Declaration, "Nostrae aeta-
tis," recognizes its involvement in the needs of our
times.

"In our times," the first sentence of the Declaration
reads, "when every day men are being drawn closer
together and the ties between various peoples are being
multiplied, the Church is giving deeper study to her
relationship with non-Christian religions."

We are here considering this dialogue insofar as it is
taking place between Christianity and Buddhism, with
particular reference to what is going on in Japan. True,
this dialogue is also occurring in other countries of
Asia, for example in Ceylon and Thailand. But I would
like to discuss the subject in its Japanese setting, because I live in that country and am personally engaged
there in the interreligious dialogue.

Traditional Japanese Buddhism is divided into numerous schools looking back on a history centuries old
and linked to China and India. In addition, there are
important "new religions" rooted in Buddhism and

connected with various lines of the tradition. Most of them derive from Nichiren, the Buddhist prophet of the Kamakura era (13th century).[2] Christian contacts exist with almost all Buddhist bodies, even with the Sōka-Gakkai, which is relatively isolated from other religions.[3] Naturally, the form of the dialogue differs according to the school or sect. Generally speaking, however, the basic beliefs of Buddhism play a more important role than the differentiated tenets of the individual sects.

In recent years, many meetings of groups and individuals of various backgrounds have taken place. There were receptions for Cardinal Marella when he visited Japan. Christian delegations attended Buddhist memorials and Buddhist delegations, Christian Mass. Catholic representatives have been present at and extended greetings to the great gathering for the celebration of Buddha's birthday in the spring. Conferences on Buddhist or Christian subjects before Christian or Buddhist audiences have been held, and finally—most important but still at an initial stage—ecumenical meetings have occurred on a scholarly level between a few selected participants.

Ecumenism, Syncretism, and Universalism

In the various contacts between Christianity and Buddhism in Japan an ecumenical attitude, eager to enter into a dialogue, induces and animates the participants. It is important, however, to grasp exactly the mode of unity intended in the particular ecumenical goal. A precise understanding is all the more important in our case because in the West, when people speak of ecumenism, they generally mean the dialogue between Christians of different denominations or churches. According to the Lord's supplication "that all may be one," the goal pursued in Christian ecumenism is Christian unity. The dialogue with non-Christian religions, however, does not have religious unity as its immediate goal, and it is necessary to recognize this. The establishment of a single world religion in which all existing religions would merge and amalgamate with one another is emphatically *not* the goal.[4] The syncretism implicit in such an idea is unacceptable not only to believers in Christianity, but also to the adherents of other religions.[5]

For, as even non-Christian religions explicitly state, no true religious conviction can exist without a claim to absolute validity. It is however true that this absolute character is perfectly compatible with religious tolerance when tolerance is correctly understood.[6]

Syncretistic unity cannot therefore constitute the objective of the dialogue. But what can we say of modern forms of the idea of unity contained in Christian universality—an essential tenet of theology since the Apostle Paul? Can they be used to promote mutual understanding in the dialogue between religions? A prominent Japanese philosopher with a Buddhist background, who takes a lively interest in the development of modern Christian theology in the Occident, has formulated the problem: Christians would no more like to be regarded as anonymous Buddhists than Buddhists like to be regarded as anonymous Christians. This of course does not argue against the vision of universality inherent in Christian theology, through the Christian's faith in the mystery of Christ. But the Christian about to start a dialogue with a non-Christian who has religious convictions of his own must himself put his Christian theological speculations in abeyance. That which is common to humanity offers the only point of departure.[7] All the same, in the actual dialogue, as we shall see, there are striking similarities between the respective religious experiences of East and West.

The First Goal of the Dialogue: Mutual Understanding and Recognition of Values

Unity is not the goal of the dialogue between Christianity and Buddhism, neither syncretistically as an integration of one religion into another, nor as a sublimation of both religions into a higher unity. The goals of the dialogue, to put it simply, are to gain and deepen mutual understanding and cooperation, on the personal level, for the common welfare of mankind. Both for understanding and for cooperation we must recognize the plurality of religions. The first goal, mutual understanding, involves a series of stages, and its implementation has many connected steps.

From the beginning, mutual understanding presupposes social intercourse in an open and congenial atmosphere. In modern society, the necessity of this first condition has been clearly demonstrated at all levels of social relations. We might rightly claim that in our century, despite the wars that have taken place, humanity has generally adopted an etiquette for social intercourse which greatly facilitates exchange and cooperation in many fields. To cite only one example, related to the interreligious dialogue, the cordial atomosphere fostered by scientific contacts has made an appreciable contribution to the realization of scientific objectives.

In Japan, there have always been good relations between Buddhists and Christians. These have been made possible by the sympathetic interest of Christians on the one hand, and by the extraordinarily ready acceptance of Christian initiatives by the Buddhists.[8] The tolerance of Japanese Buddhists is indeed amazing. The warm hospitality which awaits the non-Buddhist, even the Christian priest or monk, in a Japanese Buddhist monastery, and the readiness for religious conversation are of immeasurable help in establishing contact. If a dialogue is sincerely sought, a favorable atmosphere is there from the start. The depth of reciprocal communication, however, will depend on the depth of the religious experience of the partners in the dialogue. It may of course happen that, despite sincere friendship, the actual scope of communication will be limited.

Social gatherings are also useful in creating a favorable atmosphere. In these gatherings one can progress from uncommitted acquaintance to sympathetic friendship. Many Japanese Buddhists during their world travels met with important Christian leaders of the Occident, and not a few were unforgettably impressed by their audiences with Pope John XXIII and Pope Paul VI. It may be said that, during the last decade, many factors combined to create in Japan a desirable atmosphere for the dialogue between Buddhists and Christians.

A higher stage of mutual understanding in the dialogue comes through a knowledge of each other's values. As a matter of principle, Christians have no difficulty in recognizing the existence of religious values in non-Christian religions. The Second Vatican Council does this explicitly in its "Declaration on the Relationship of the Church to Non-Christian Religions." The statement of the Council reaffirms the rich tradition of Christian humanism which goes back in antiquity to

Justin and Lactantius, Clement of Alexandria and Origen, which was alive in Augustine and Thomas Aquinas, and which in modern times particularly influenced Francis de Sales, Fénelon and Newman. The truths contained in non-Christian religions testify to God's work of salvation in the whole of mankind. Modern Christian theology attempts to define more precisely than in the past the significance of the non-Christian religions in the divine plan of salvation, but often this attempt is confined to general considerations and does not pay sufficient attention to the specific nature of the various non-Christian religions. These general considerations remain within the sphere of theological speculation. For the concrete dialogue, however, the cardinal problem is to recognize and esteem the particular and individual values of the other religions.

These values in turn illuminate the great religious minds of the non-Christian world and the movements or institutions descending from them. In God's plan of salvation for mankind, the Eastern sages Confucius, Lao-tzu and the Buddha are certainly no less important than Socrates, Plato or Aristotle. Once we come to the actual dialogue, the major weakness of the so-called "theology of religions" is that it is too general to do justice to the immense complexity of the phenomena of non-Christian religions and their historical origins.[9]

An accurate knowledge of other religions is necessary for the dialogue. Naturally, the dialogue ought to correct, supplement and enrich this knowledge. But a certain preliminary understanding is the indispensable prerequisite for a useful dialogue. Interest and study are required to fulfill this condition, and only a limited number of adherents of the various religions will be able to qualify. The knowledge of the history of religions now transmitted by general school education is entirely insufficient. It is not easy to evaluate the educated Buddhist's knowledge of Christianity. The esteem for Christianity, often coupled with sympathy, usually far surpasses actual knowledge about Christian matters. The interest of Christians in other religions, notably in Buddhism, has increased remarkably in recent years. But knowledge is sufficient in rare cases only, partly on account of the difficulty of the subject, partly because Eastern thinking is so entirely different from Western thinking. This insufficiency has been recognized, and suitable ways of remedying the situation are being explored.[10]

By itself, knowledge (even accurate, comprehensive and precise knowledge) is of little avail unless it is supported by a human feeling for and insight into the real intent and values of other religions. Since Buddhism, in the course of its long history, has developed numerous branches, its values cannot easily be reduced to a simple formula. However, the Second Vatican Council, in its declaration on the attitude of the Church toward non-Christian religions, enumerated in summary at least the most important basic religious values of Buddhism. The text of the declaration mentions (1) the acknowledgment of the radical insufficiency of this shifting world, (2) the devout and confident spirit, and (3) the desire for a state of absolute freedom (this paraphrases Nirvāna, the final goal as taught in original Buddhism and in today's southern Theravāda Buddhism), or for supreme enlightenment (in the Mahāyāna Buddhism of East Asia). In the final form of the document the latter goal, at the request of the Japanese bishops, was more specifically described as one to be attained "by their (i.e., men's) own efforts" (*jiriki*) or "with outside help" (*tariki*)—the two ways of salvation represented in the two main forms of Japanese Buddhism, the Zen schools and the Amida schools. The conciliar text, by indicating these essential elements of Buddhism, offers possible points of departure for a dialogue with Buddhism.[11]

This brief and incomplete enumeration, however, only provides the Christian partner in the dialogue with directions for the further exploration of the terrain. He will have to examine the realization of values in the daily religious life of the Buddhist and try to understand correctly his religious practices. In doing so, he may become increasingly aware of the actual meaning and specifically religious content in the life of the Buddhist, and thereby approach the area in which he may discover links with his own Christian devotion. He may thus perceive the "common ground" of which Pope John XXIII spoke to a group of Japanese Buddhists in that memorable meeting on 18 November 1962.

A major concern for the Christian partner in the dialogue will be to ensure that the attitude of his Buddhist partner does not stop at a general esteem for Christianity, often mixed with a deep respect for Western civilization. The Buddhist must also arrive at an understanding of the specific values of Christianity. Many of these values—in particular, those that today are called structurally Christian—have found entry into Japan together with Western civilization, among them, the values of the individual, of social justice, equality and fraternity.[12] The general Japanese public hardly, if at all, thinks of structurally Christian values as something Christian. It must be regarded all the more remarkable, therefore, that Sōka-Gakkai, the largest numerically and the most active of the Japanese new religions (which has its origin in Nichiren Buddhism) vindicates its engagement in democratic politics by pointing expressly to the line of action of Christian

politicians and Christian political parties in Europe
(particularly in West Germany, Italy and Switzerland).
On several occasions, including an interview for the
renowned Japanese literary magazine *Bungei Shunjū,*
Daisaku Ikeda, Sōka-Gakkai's president, justified his
religion's "politics based on faith" by referring to Christian sociology and political science.[13] Here is a case
where a religion, often regarded as intolerant, seems to
have established at least a remote relationship with
Christianity.

But what about the recognition of Christian religious
values in the proper sense, different from and beyond
the structurally Christian, humanitarian values? A dialogue must take into account the fact that these values
are less intelligible to Buddhism, that the most basic
values of Christian religious life (above all the belief in
one God, the Creator) are far removed from the Buddhist religious consciousness. It should be remembered
that for Eastern man, experience is the alpha and the
omega of religious life. No theoretical doctrines, no
discussions about truths, can inaugurate an interreligious dialogue in Asia. Only the actual religious life
lived by Christians can lead Japanese Buddhists to a
deeper understanding of the Christian religion.

The Christian version of religious life is prayer. I do
not assert that Christian prayer is immediately and
readily accessible to Japanese Buddhists. Certainly not.
But not infrequently, Japanese Buddhists evince a very
vivid interest in Christian prayer, not out of theoretical
curiosity, but because they conjecture that its values
enrich religious life. As a matter of fact, some of the
Japanese new religions—for example, the Buddhist inspired Risshō Kōseikai movement—have introduced
responsive prayer into their religious practice, although

this was unknown to traditional Japanese Buddhism. In addition to the recitation of sutras and the invocation of the Holy Name, the Risshō Kōseikai teach the faithful to recite morning and evening prayers in set formulas addressed to the Buddha, to a Bodhisattva, or to the chief objects of veneration of the religious community. These new religions, which make their members religiously active, have been said to reveal a monotheistic tendency. If such a tendency actually exists, it does not have a theoretical foundation, but derives from the practical propensity for personification. For example, President Ikeda of Sōka-Gakkai invoked with supreme religious intensity the "principal object of worship" (*Go Honzon*), which is identical with Saint Nichiren or, according to the monistic metaphysics of Mahāyāna Buddhism, with the Eternal All-Buddha: "Go Honzon, let me accomplish this today! Today, I want to do this!" or, "I have the responsibility of a struggle. Let me put forth my entire strength!" [14]

In the case of the new religions, it is not easy to determine the degree and manner of Christian influence, nor to decide whether it is derived from structurally Christian values, or more or less directly from the religious content of Christianity, or whether it is the work of the *anima naturaliter Christiana.*

Most Japanese new religions of Buddhist lineage maintain a relationship permitting dialogue with Christianity. In many cases, the general syncretistic tendency of these religions leads to a sincere desire to learn something good and useful from Christianity. Their practice, however, also contains mechanical, schematic and even shamanistic elements. A certain reserve, therefore, is advisable in evaluating the reception of Christian values into their religious practices.

Understanding Based on Experience: The Oiso Conference

Having made this reservation, we now come to the higher stage of mutual understanding based on deep religious experience. The most important meeting between Christians and Buddhists held so far in Japan was a conference arranged by the Quakers and directed by Dr. Douglas V. Steere, who had been an Observer at Vatican II. It took place in the Protestant Academy House at Oiso, near Tokyo, from 27 March to 1 April 1967, and brought about an intimate spiritual contact. The Christians included both Protestants and Catholics; the Buddhists belonged to the two principal Japanese schools of Zen Buddhism, Rinzai and Sōtō. Both groups included men engaged in actual religious service at Buddhist temples and Christian churches, as well as university professors and scholars. Throughout the meeting, the participants lived together as an intimate personal community. I was among them. In the morning, we discussed two major themes, "My Spiritual Way," and "Religion's Responsibility for Modern Society." Personal religious experience thus stood in the foreground of the dialogue, and we were given an opportunity to see how important personal experience is for deeper mutual understanding.

The Spiritual Way

First, the Protestant theologian Kazō Kitamori sought to explain to the participants his road to Christianity through personal devotion, fostered in the home of his Buddhist parents. The Christian belief in God freed him from the existential anxiety of searching for the meaning of life, while his experience of man's sinfulness drew him to Christ the Mediator and Redeemer. Christ's cross revealed God's infinite love in the form of the suffering of God. This basic religious experience laid the foundation for his Lutheran-oriented treatise on grace and justification, *Theology of the Pain of God.* This work, already known in the United States, may well rank as the most impressive and original contemporary Japanese formulation of faith in Christ.[15]

In a somewhat different way, sin and the cross stood at the center of the experience of Christ for two Protestant theologians from the Free Church movement of Japan. Both are eminent biblical scholars who studied in Germany: Masao Sekine specializes in the Old Testament, Seiichi Yagi in the New. Sekine spoke of his conversion and inner transformation, in which he experienced the theological truth of the unity of justification and sanctification in the new creation of man through Christ. Today, however, he finds it difficult to bring his personal experience of Christian existence into accord with the biblical science to which he devotes himself heart and soul. The same difficulty also troubles his younger colleague, Seiichi Yagi.[16]

The Protestant theologians related the theology of the cross to the religious experience of the non-ego in Buddhism. The death of the selfish "I," the work of the grace of Christ's death on the cross, can, they believe, be compared to the renunciation of the subjective "I" in the enlightenment of Zen Buddhism. This analogy was stressed particularly in Yagi's report on his encounter with Zen Buddhism. For Kitamori, the conquest of all forms of dualism constitutes the main religious achievement of Buddhism. His Lutheran theology of the cross aims at an absolute unity, excluding every

kind of dualism. Eastern thought, he believes, will ena-
ble Christian theology to gain a deeper insight into the
mystery of the unity in God and Christ.

In their reports on the interior way, the Catholic
participants focused their attention on the experience
of prayer strictly defined. They attempted to clarify the
relationship between their own specifically Christian
prayer and Zen meditation. The three Catholic reports
on this subject agreed that no unbridgeable gap exists
between the two spiritual ways. The first report stressed
the complementarity of the two ways characteristic of
the difference in attitude of East and West: silent meditation on the one hand, and prayer as dialogue on the
other. In actual practice, these two attitudes hardly
occur in pure and exclusive forms. Although Christian
spirituality begins by teaching recollection in the presence of God, conversation with God, and personal encounter with God, it leads in the subsequent stages of
prayer to stillness, deep silence and perfect simplicity,
in which the divine mystery is experienced as superper-
sonal infinite love. The mystery of God, which the soul
touches upon in its higher stages of prayer, transcends
all words and concepts. Based on these experiences,
Christian spirituality brought forth the "negative theology" whose fundamental intent is akin to the Eastern
way of negation (*mu.*)[17]

Ichirō Okumura, a young Japanese Carmelite priest,
genuinely combined the noblest values of the Japanese
tradition with a deep understanding of Carmelite
spirituality. He became acquainted with the Carmelite
tradition through the works of St. John of the Cross
soon after his baptism, and later he chose it as his own
way. When he entered the Carmelite Order, he took
with him his earlier experience in the practice of Zen
and his intimate familiarity with the writings of the

great Zen master, Dōgen. He is bound to the traditional way of prayer of his Order but, at the same time, believes that Zen meditation can enrich Christian spirituality because it is aware of the unity of body and soul in man, and effectively practices "prayer with the body." For in perfect prayer, the "whole man" prays, "with his head, his heart and his body."

On the final day, H. M. Enomiya-Lassalle, whose knowledge of Zen meditation is unrivalled, further discussed the relationship between Zen practice and Christianity. He was led to the practice of Zen not by any personal religious crisis or doubts about Christianity, but by the desire to penetrate more deeply into the Japanese mentality, where Zen has played such a decisive role. From his actual experience of Zen meditation, he became convinced that Zen offered the possibility of overcoming certain difficulties which he has long encountered in the traditional methods of prayer widely used in Christianity. He was, of course, acquainted with Christian mysticism; but in Christianity, the mystical way somehow seemed hardly accessible. In his first attempt at Zen meditation, he felt a new possiblity of progress in spiritual concentration and recollection, a possibility which, up until then, had been completely unknown to him, yet which, he felt, could and should be of the utmost importance for Christian prayer. Thus he entered the way of Zen practice, and those of the participants familiar with Zen could understand the heroic resolve and unwearied patience which this required. He mentioned only the necessity of placing himself under the direction of a Zen master. His report clearly showed the value of the practice of Zen for Christian spirituality.[18]

The reports of the Zen Buddhists, less homogeneous than those of the Christian participants, cannot easily be put in any particular order. There were straight-forward accounts of the speaker's own religious development, relating the inner growth of Buddhist piety, the penetration of religious convictions into the individual's life, and the deepening of inner life through practice and study. Different from these accounts were the reports of participants whose religious views had been influenced by Zen Buddhism, but whose convictions matured outside the framework of Buddhist institutions. A unique place, finally, must be assigned to the report of the Zen master, Yamada Mumon; his was the only account illustrating Zen enlightenment as actually experienced and lived by a *rōshi*.

Two things were characteristic for the first set of reports. First, there were accounts of the experience of renouncing the world, born out of the realization of the transience of earthly things and the value of the things of the spirit. And there were accounts of the experience of enlightenment in everyday life—in the midst of a full and busy working day with an almost uninterrupted sequence of problems and vexations, difficulties and annoyances from morning to night. The only thing that could bring freedom and peace of mind, declared an overburdened university president and Zen master, is the sustained practice of Zen, the breath of enlightenment or Great Nature, with which the disciple of Zen becomes one.[19] The cosmic experience of becoming one with the universe, typical of Zen, somehow anticipates death and imparts the feeling of being sheltered in a depth enfolding man like the womb of a mother. Man finds himself in harmony; nothing can dismay him. Whenever adversity meets him, he falls back on the practice of rhythmic breathing. The solution to all difficulties lies in breathing, in the uninterrupted continuation of Zen meditation in everyday life.

Another renowned participant was Professor Masao Abe, himself not a Buddhist monk but linked to Zen Buddhism through his religious and scholarly achievement. His whole life has been dominated by an earnest and self-denying quest for truth. His family professed the Buddhism of the Shin sect and, in his younger years, his fervent desire for salvation found expression in the invocation of the holy name of the Buddha (*nembutsu*). This practice, followed by the adherents of the Amida sects, is characteristic of the way of salvation "with outside help" (*tariki*) and considered as the "easy way" in the history of Japanese religions.[20] But the true *nembutsu*, Professor Abe explained, is quite difficult. For in the truthful invocation of Buddha's name, the mere movement of the lips is completely useless. Neither is it a matter of personal exertion. The true *nembutsu* means identification with the Amida Buddha's "Original Vow" (*hongan*) to save all living beings. Obviously, this interpretation of *nembutsu* approaches the religious point of view of Zen Buddhism. But the way of Zen leads beyond *nembutsu* and, by overcoming all dualism, ends in creative and absolute freedom. Professor Abe formulated Zen's religious version of monism with great clarity; but his own religious journey does not seem to have reached its final goal. As he indicated in the discussion following his report, his quest and questioning continue. He is intensely interested in what he calls "original Buddhism," not the historical beginnings of Buddhism but its quintessence. At the same time, however, he is engaged in an inner dialogue with Christianity; for ever since his boyhood, he has thought a great deal about the meaning of grace and "salvation by higher assistance."

The participant most representative of the only distinctively Japanese philosophical school, the so-called

Kyoto School, was Professor Toratarō Shimomura. The Kyoto School, which owes much to Zen,[21] was founded by Kitarō Nishida and Hajime Tanabe; Shimomura, who teaches philosophy, is one of their immediate disciples. In the beginning of his report, Shimomura remarked that he does not adhere to religious Buddhism. Like so many of his countrymen, particularly the intellectuals, he remains without definite beliefs, "outside the gate" of religion. Unlike many others, however, he is (as he himself emphasized) by no means indifferent to religion. Still, he could never bring himself to join with any religious institution, despite his close contacts with Buddhism during his student days in Kyoto, and with Christianity as an instructor at Christian schools. If asked what his relationship to Buddhism was, he could not claim, he said, to be a Buddhist but neither could he deny that he was a Buddhist. This statement is intelligible because the name "Buddhist" does not imply sharply drawn boundaries. This, as Shimomura said, is one of the important differences between Buddhism and Christianity, or even between Far Eastern and Western religions in general. In Western Christianity, doctrine predominates, whereas in Japan, religion is a "way." In the discussion that followed, Shimomura further specified his reservations about Christianity: they deserve serious attention because they are shared by many Japanese intellectuals. He particularly deprecated Christianity's antagonistic attitude toward other religions and denominations which, he said, in the West often went as far as religious wars and which showed itself in Asiatic countries in the Christian attempt to absorb other religions, traditions and cultures.

The final report to the conference had been reserved for the Zen Master, Yamada Mumon. He began with a simple narrative of his childhood and his student days, his early contacts with Confucian wisdom and Christianity. He then spoke of his resolve to renounce the world, and formulated his motive for becoming a monk in words expressing the Bodhisattva ideal of Mahāyāna Buddhism: "to sacrifice oneself and serve mankind." He must have felt the proximity of this attitude to Christian ideals, for he explicitly noted the similarity between the image of Bodhisattva and the image of Christ.

His undertaking first led him into a dark night of soul and body both. Severe illness forced him to leave the extremely strict Buddhist monastery that he had entered. Back at home he endured months of physical pain, loneliness and complete desolation. One spring day he dragged himself to the veranda of his parents' house. A gentle breeze softly caressed his skin. "What is the wind? What is the air? Am I ever really alone? Am I not always surrounded by wind and air?" Deep inside he felt himself sustained by an ever-present sublime being. This conviction gave him the strength to devote himself once again to the practice of Zen. This time he took up the therapy which the well known Zen Master Hakuin used and recommended to his disciples.[22] After regaining his health, he turned to authentic Zen practices and one day, while contemplating some brilliant red maple leaves, found enlightenment.

Master Mumon described enlightenment as the moment of total self-oblivion, of knowing without knowing and seeing without seeing, in which being is born out of nothingness. His comments contained an observation which I found surprising, though it is typical and deserves our attention. Several times he spoke in a sympathetic manner of his relation to Christianity, and he mentioned particularly his respect for the Bible. But formal prayers, as they are used in Christian churches, seem to him entirely inappropriate. Prayer as dialogue is alien to the completely introverted Zen master.

Religious Responsibility

The second subject discussed by the conference, the necessary and complementary pole of the first theme, brought the participants face to face with the needs and crises of our time. In dealing with the responsibility of religion for the world, the discussions assumed greater importance than the reports themselves. It was only in the exchange of views that the real problems involved in this topic became clear. And despite lengthy debates, certain issues remained unresolved. In view of the complexity of the problems this was hardly a surprise. The main lines of thought which emerged from the reports and discussions may be summarized under three headings: (1) the relationship between a religious attitude based on experience and social service, (2) responsibility for shaping new social structures adapted to the present time, and (3) specific social issues, in particular the problem of world peace.

In the course of the discussions, there appeared considerable differences on specific issues; but a basic agreement prevailed with regard to the responsibility of religion for the world's social order. True, Professor Shōkin Furuta, a historian and a disciple of D. T. Suzuki of the Rinzai School, propounded the view that Buddhism, and particularly Zen Buddhism, has no direct mission for social works. He admitted that Buddhism has a cultural and spiritual function but argued that as exemplified in the great religious reformers, Dōgen and Shinran, it has no immediate task in the field of social activities. The mission of religion, he contended, was confined to the religious sphere in the strict sense. In the case of Zen Buddhism, this means that everything depends on the radical renunciation of the world and the ego, and the attainment of enlightenment. In this connection, Furuta quoted the old Japanese saying: "Go into the mountain and come out of the mountain."

In the discussions following, this phrase was often repeated. All the participants agreed that true religious service to man and society was impossible without the solitude of the mountain, that is, without dying to the world outwardly and inwardly. But there was also a consensus of opinion that the combination of going into and coming out of the mountain—in Christian terminology, the union of contemplation and action—was difficult to accomplish. Master Mumon deplored the fact that nowadays many Buddhists went "into the mountain" but, out of a general lack of a strong sense of social responsibility, neglected to return to serve society. In his conception of Buddhism, everyone who attains true enlightenment returns to society and social service.

The Zen Buddhists of the Oiso conference insisted on the preeminence of enlightenment (*satori*) and the priority of inner fulfillment over external activity. This naturally raised the question whether an essential relationship exists between the experience of enlightenment and social service. Does responsibility for one's fellow man (and society) belong to the essence of the religious experience? The question is posed in the same terms for the Buddhist as for the Christian. It was agreed that the Christian position needed no answer. The discussion, therefore, focused on Zen Buddhism. Master Yamada Mumon explained the Buddhist position in detail. He referred to the story of the meeting of St. Francis of Assisi with the leper, and remarked that it was not the alms but the embrace which saved the leper. To give money or other material things is the minimum; to call forth gratitude is more. The enlightened person gives himself and thereby everything. Enlightenment overcomes all duality, eliminates the separation from the other, creates unity. The enlightened person himself experiences complete unity in which he is one with the other. The other is his self, just as the mountain is his self and the flower is his self. Whoever has attained enlightenment renders service to his fellow man as a matter of course, because there is no separation between his own self and the other. To base social service on the identity of the self and the other experienced in enlightenment, is not necessarily to exclude the personal value of the individual or his fellow man. But ultimately, this basis rests within the cosmic order. It would seem, therefore, that the basic Buddhist virtue of compassion as sympathy with all living beings (*jihi*), taught by the Buddha himself, provides a more effective foundation for social service. During the conference, this compassion was frequently mentioned, but its significance for social service was not sufficiently emphasized. Buddhism today may stand in need of spiritual aid, if compassion is to become the point of departure for service to modern society.[23]

When choosing the subject of religion's responsibility for the world, the planners of the conference thought particularly of the complex of problems involving the responsibility of religion for the new social structures required by the technical era. Without such structures, mankind's spiritual culture, indispensable to true human happiness, may be in serious jeopardy. These problems were frequently touched upon but in general the discussion did not go beyond suggestions and hints which, unfortunately, were not fully accepted or thoroughly explored.

The Japanese Dominican, Shigeto Oshida, not only made an earnest appeal for social service—necessary if religions are to be credible in the eyes of our contemporaries—but also described his vision of a new world and a new social order to be built by all men of good will in a common effort. Only a new comprehensive blueprint for a better world based on religion can engage the energies of the young generation. Oshida's appeal made a deep impression on the participants; the young Zen Buddhists particularly were deeply moved by it.

Two Zen Buddhists, Eshin Nishimura and Takashi Hirata, stressed the dynamic potential of historical reality as an essential element of man's existence. A critical evaluation of history leads to freedom and constitutes an important task of our times. To fulfill his mission in a constantly changing world, man must live in a present moment whose character is determined by history. Religion's service to mankind requires a constant effort at a dynamic adaptation to historical reality.

Religion's responsibility for the preservation of world peace was the only specific issue related to the second topic of the conference and was discussed by the participants because of the urgency of the problem, Junichi Asano, who belongs to the older generation of Japanese Protestant theologians, called on the conference to define its position on war. Needless to say, all the participants agreed to the urgent need for working together toward the goal of world peace.

The Oiso conference was the first large-scale interreligious meeting in Japan.[24] Pope John XXIII's dictum of "the common ground on which all religions rest," was often cited throughout the conference. In his closing address, the Zen Abbot Shibayama Zenkei spoke earnestly of his experience of what was common to all religions and the obligation of all religions for mutual understanding. This prepared the way for a last discussion on the "common ground." A number of participants would have welcomed a verbal formulation, perhaps through philosophy, where the Kyoto School approximates certain tendencies in Western philosophy. But the search for explicit formulation was futile. There can be no doubt about the common ground of all religions, but it cannot be grasped in words.

The claim of Christianity to absoluteness and universality is founded on the event and the fact of Christ. Non-Christians, of course, do not accept this fact. Thus in dialogue, no appeal to the incorporation of non-Christians into the reality of Christ (for instance, as anonymous Christians)[25] can be made. A Christian who, in recognition of the values implied in non-Christian religions, would try to convince his non-Christian partner that his values were actually Christian, or that he himself was tacitly a Christian, would meet not only with incomprehension but with deep resentment. Nothing is more irritating to the religiously minded Asian non-Christian, to a Buddhist or Hindu in particular, than what to him is a typically Christian arrogance of trying to incorporate and absorb all other religions. In his attitude toward dialogue, the Christian must take the "otherness" of the others seriously. The ecumenical encounter with non-Christians can neither intend their conversion nor the transmutation of their beliefs into Christian conceptions; still less can it aim toward some kind of syncretism or sublimation into a higher unity. The situation should be one wherein we are conscious of the common ground and sincerely desire a deeper mutual understanding with inner respect and sympathy; where we talk with each other in order to learn from each other and, whenever possible, cooperate for the welfare of mankind. But the conviction of the common ground, important as it is, should not obscure the necessity of respect for real differences.

This recognition of differences may still be compatible with a point of departure which can push the dialogue a step further. I have often noticed that Buddhists of the most different schools possessed an experience of the Absolute as the Supreme Being or, at least, that they sincerely sought such an experience. They desired to learn more about the Christian experience of the Infinite, known to many of them through the Bible, above all the Gospel of St. John. That many Christian insights are buried under external observance and are difficult to detect comes as no surprise to them. Even in today's Buddhism, external functions predominate. In their discussions with Christians, Japanese Buddhists are ready to set aside all conceptual systems and to search for inner meaning. The transcendence and otherness of the Supreme Being bar conceptual access. In 1967 I had ample opportunity to meet leading Buddhists in Korea, where present political and cultural conditions allow only a restricted dialogue between Christians and Buddhists. In a lecture at the Buddhist Dong-kuk University in Seoul, I spoke on "negative theology" in the Christian Bible in connection with the Mahāyāna doctrine of the cosmic Buddha. The rapprochement touched the innermost core of religion: human knowledge of Absolute Being. The reaction of the audience showed that the experienced Mahāyāna Buddhists possess a living contact with the Absolute, confirming Pascal's word, "Thou wouldst not seek me if thou hadst not found me!"

The Second Goal of the Dialogue: Cooperation

The second important goal of the interreligious dialogue between Buddhism and Christianity is cooperation. In principle, the will to cooperate exists on both sides in Japan, and the prevailing friendly atmosphere makes common action easier. In the first place there are common organizational arrangements. All religious bodies in Japan belong to an association which operates with little friction and achieves satisfactory results.[26] The organizational collaboration permits common action in dealing with the authorities, above all with the Ministry of Education, in such things as legal measures or the promotion of general undertakings of a social or charitable nature.

In a country like Japan, one possible goal for cooperation among religious organizations would be to secure a place in public life for their activities. Since the end of the war, many Japanese religious groups have developed a sense of solidarity in seeking this goal, but the practical effect of this solidarity has been extremely limited. Greater effort is required if the religious groups want to bring their demands and aspirations to the attention of the public.[27]

Social cooperation between Buddhists and Christians rests on a religious foundation for which the two religions use different names (the Christians call it charity, the Buddhists sympathetic compassion), but which is essentially the same in both. What the Christian does in charity and what the Buddhist does in compassion, reveals the profound goodness which can dwell in man's heart and which bears witness to the Eternal Love above man. As with the life of meditation, works of charity and compassion can bring Buddhists and Christians together in a real and living way.

Today, cooperation for preserving world peace is a common task of all religions. For the Buddhists, the very essence of their religion constitutes the basis of its mission for peace. The founder of Buddhism, Shākya-muni, lives in the memory of his believers as the harbinger of peace, and his message preached absolute pardon and reconciliation. More than anything else, the Occident's bloodied ecclesiastical history with its ruthless religious wars is apt to cause distrust and even hostility against Christianity; but the sincere peace efforts of the recent popes have found a sympathetic echo in the hearts of the faithful among all schools of Buddhism in Japan. If religiously motivated, the quest for peace can more than any other objective unite Buddhists and Christians in common action.

Since the atomic holocausts of Hiroshima and Nagasaki, Japan has been conscious of her particular obligation for maintaining world peace. Japan's solicitude for peace finds solid support in the two world religions, Christianity and Buddhism, which especially can be regarded as religions of peace. Both religions are well aware of their mission for peace; and the manifestations of this awareness run through the various dialogue-events sponsored by Christians and Buddhists. At the beginning of 1968, Buddhists attended prayer meetings for world peace in the Catholic cathedral in Tokyo,[28] and Christians joined Buddhists in offering incense and praying in Buddhist temples for all victims of the war in Vietnam. These actions are more than mere gestures, for such a communion leaves a deep impression in the consciousness of the participants.

The World Conference for Religion and Peace, which took place in Kyoto, Japan's former capital and seat of the Emperor, from 16 to 22 October 1970, covered a wider ground. Over 300 representatives of large and small religious groups took part. The conference, international in tone, looked beyond Asia to touch upon most of the important questions concerning interreligious cooperation for the welfare of mankind. Japan's "peace-constitution," whose 9th Article expressly rejects war as a means to resolve international conflicts, was mentioned in connection with recent efforts to amend the national constitution. There is no lack of votes in Japan to change a constitution which some believe unrealistic in today's armed world. Thus, as the late Professor Wilhelm Schiffer of Sophia University reported, there were heated arguments between the "realistic" Japanese Buddhists and the more "idealistic" Japanese Protestants.[29] The general atmosphere of the conference, fortunately congenial even if at times controversial, made it clear to the participants that there is dire need for mutual consideration of common problems. And despite the many pertinent and even daring statements aimed toward politicians and statesmen alike, there remained the question whether the statesmen of the world will heed the contention of religions.

Still, immediate results in the realm of politics are not the ultimate issue. Rather the point is that the religions of the world must not stint their efforts toward peace and the welfare of mankind. Mutual cooperation in Japan, particularly between Buddhists and Christians, is already taking place. Archbishop Shirayanagi of

Tokyo serves as an example of this mutual effort. At a meeting of Asian bishops in Manila in November 1970, on the occasion of Pope Paul VI's visit to Asia and Australia, the Archbishop remarked that "Our experiences . . . have confirmed our conviction that not only Christians but men of other religions share a common concern for development and that in this pursuit of social justice we should all be together." It can safely be said that cooperation for world peace and social justice will unite Buddhists and Christians in Asia for a long time to come.

The Extent and Modern Character of the Dialogue

Because of the multiplicity of the religious groups engaged, the dialogue between Christianity and Buddhism in Japan is of considerable scope. It necessarily comes into contact with the movement for modernization in Japanese Buddhism. This movement, common to traditional Buddhism and the new religions derived from it, aims at adapting Buddhism to the needs of our time consistent with the modernization and Westernization of Japan's national culture. Rationalizing, demythologizing, democratizing, and social action are among the most prominent tendencies, drawing their main inspiration from a modern humanism which asserts the personal values of man. It is evident that, through such efforts, Buddhist schools and sects of all descriptions are brought nearer to the humanistic features of Christianity.

A study conference organized by the Secretariat for the Dialogue with Non-Believers took place in Tokyo from 2 to 4 June 1969, and dealt with the subject "Secularization and Atheism in Asia."[30] It arrived at the note-worthy conclusion that the secularizing tendencies now at work in all Asian countries can create new possibilities for the dialogue of Christianity with non-Christian religions. For a correct understanding of this unexpected result, two points should be made. First, secularization, inasmuch as it involves the development of human potentialities and human culture, is regarded in Asia as an eminently positive process, and deserves to be recognized as valuable from a Christian point of view as well. Antireligious, militantly atheistic or anticlerical elements play only a subordinate role today. Second, because of the decisive influence of technological progress, of industrialization and urban growth, secularization not only liberates man's religious life from much that is unsound, superstitious, and magical, but also breaks down nationalistic antagonism to the West and Western culture. Because it furthers the contacts with world civilization, secularization often completes the spiritual emancipation from colonialism and makes a voluntary opening to Christian values possible.

Moreover, because of its connection with modernization in general, secularization helps to uncover the common human ground in all religions. This aspect stands out prominently in modern Japan, where the non-Christian religions interpret and practice modernization as humanization. The humanistic tendency can be regarded as the leading idea in the modernization of Japanese Buddhism, and this tendency again gives rise to other secularizing measures, such as the turn to this world and the emphasis on social service.[31] Significantly, social responsibility has moved into the foreground in the countries of Theravāda Buddhism as well—for example, in Thailand and Ceylon. In its doctrine, Theravāda Buddhism is rather individualistic; its religious practice is directed toward personal salvation and the individual acquisition of merit. Today, however, under the influence of a new interpretation of religion, religiously valuable and meritorious activity is no longer restricted to almsgiving for the support of monks and temples, but has been extended to include efforts for the welfare of the people—as for example increase in production.

In this regard, the turn of present day Buddhism to its origins, which is occurring along with modernization and secularization, deserves special attention. Not only is this turning point in the modern Buddhist movement of great importance for the unity of international Buddhism; it also opens up new possibilities for resolving the issues of the times within Buddhism. The more universal a religion is, the more easily and effectively it can adapt to the changing needs of the times.[32] In turning back to its beginnings, Buddhism is retrieving its original universal character and this character is essentially humanistic. Thus the turn to original Buddhism is fusing with the discovery of humane values in the widespread movement of secularization and modernization. The view of many historians of religion—that Buddhism is a religion which negates the world and turns to the mystic regions within oneself, and thus is incompatible with today's sensitivity—is thereby shown to be misleading.[33] On the contrary, the religion of the Buddha serves as a paragon of an ancient yet renewable tradition which today can transmit welcome and very needed values. We have already emphasized how important this occurrence is for a Christian-Buddhist encounter. The impulses coming from secularization and modernization shape new religious conceptions which manifestly can prepare a new rapport with Christianity.[34]

Asia and Europe: Background and Significance of the Christian-Buddhist Encounter

As part of the general encounter between East and West, Asia and Europe, the dialogue between Christianity and Buddhism assumes a wider meaning. To the historian, it offers a fascinating spectacle of secular as well as religious importance. More than two thousand years ago, Eastern spirituality in the form of Buddhism met Western culture for the first time when Alexander the Great fought his way to India and his successors planted Hellenistic culture on both sides of the Khyber Pass, in the Kabul Valley, and on the heights of Taxila. Widespread excavations, which are still going on, have revealed the impact of those events. The union of Greek mind and Asian spirit occurred in spacious stone monasteries or Vihāras. There, thousands of Buddhist monks, while devoting themselves to an ascetic life and contemplation, grew to know the Hellenism brought to them by mercenary armies of mixed ethnic origin but of the same Hellenistic culture. Thus the Indo-Greek culture came to influence the entire history of Buddhism in Asia; its artistic influence is still visible in the celebrated Buddhist works of art of the Nara period. The intercourse between East and West resulted in the reception of certain Graeco-Occidental values into Buddhism. In the opposite direction, although Indo-Buddhist spirituality was known in the Occident at the time of Christ, it had as yet hardly penetrated the culture. But Eastern meditation probably influenced Christian mysticism through the gateways of Alexandria and Neoplatonism, and the influence was retained and handed down through the ages.[35]

That first encounter between the religion of Buddha and the Occident on Indian frontiers was without doubt the most interesting and probably the most significant encounter until the present day. Later, in medieval times, Nestorian Christians pushed their way into central Asia and as far as China. The lengthy contact that was thus established between Christians and Buddhists also deserves our attention. The Nestorians arrived in China around 631, and their presence is documented as late as the 14th century. An inscription on a monument erected in 781 indicates how close relations were between the Nestorian "missionaries" and Chinese Buddhists. Not only did Buddhists and Christians erect the so-called "Nestorian Monument" in friendly collaboration, but it appears from the inscription that the Nestorians were more influenced by Buddhism than the Buddhists by Christianity.[36]

Among the many Buddhist schools in China at that time, Amidism and the Tantric School of the "True Word" are of special importance in the search for possible Christian influence. In both cases, research has as yet not been able to verify any direct transmission of Christian elements, and one must not overestimate Christian influence through the Nestorians. This is particularly the case with Amidism, which, because of its amazing spiritual similarity to Christianity, has often been the subject of conjecture concerning a direct Christian influence.[37]

Nestorians in China cannot be regarded the bearers of a Christian influence for the reason that Amidism was essentially developed by the time Nestorianism found its way to China. As can easily be shown, the

main elements of the religion of Amida are already
found in the two basic Pure Land Sutras,[38] which originated most probably in India in the 2nd century A.D.
The history of religions is prone to explain both the
figure of the Buddha Amitābha (Japanese: *Amida*)—
often seen as a monotheistic figure—and the elsewhere
nonexistent emphasis on faith and devotion, as stemming from the milieu in which the religion of Amida
emerged. The figure of the highest Buddha Amitābha
as "infinite light" probably stems from Iran,[39] while the
devotional aspect of this school of the Pure Land is seen
as an influence from the *bhakti* devotion which blos-
somed in India about the time of Christ. Yet there is
no evidence against the supposition that elements like
faith, trusting surrender, veneration, and so on were
intensified through the intimate contact between Amida
devotees and Nestorian Christians.

In summary then, it is true that one must not suppose
too readily that the teachings and the practice of Amida
Buddhism and Christianity were directly dependent
upon each other. Yet the amazing convergence of
Amida faith and Christian piety during the centuries
of cohabitation of China by Amida Buddhists and Nestorian Christians, might well have had a profound impact on the powerful expansion of the Amida religion
in East Asia.

The journeys of Franciscan missionaries and of the
Venetian Marco Polo to China, in the 13th and 14th
centuries, occurred near the end of the medieval period
of Buddhist-Christian contact. From their reports we
gather that they did their best to further the good atmosphere they found in the court of the Manchu emperor in Peking.[40] It is all the more regrettable, therefore, that the overthrow of the Yuan dynasty in the
latter half of the 14th century brought a quick and

complete end to the friendly relations between Buddhists and Christians in China.

The annals of modern Christian missionaries in China report no further significant encounters with Buddhism. The predominant locus of modern contact has been Japan. And here it has been the Zen school of meditation which plays the most important role. The encounter of Christian missionaries in Japan with Zen Buddhists during the so-called "Christian Century" (from the middle of the 16th century to the beginning of the 17th century) will be touched upon in the next chapter. Suffice it to say here that the Occident has pressed for contact with Asia, its spiritual heritage and its ancient religions since the earliest times. Impulses from the West occurred at different times and often came to a standstill. Yet they can serve to place the Buddhist-Christian dialogue of today in its true historical context.

Notes

1   Since the Second Vatican Council, the dialogue has evolved in full breadth in four areas—inside the Church, with other Christian communities, with non-Christian religions, and with non-believers. Of these four, the dialogue with non-Christian religions may well be the least advanced because the necessary contacts are just now being established in the countries in question. The Council provided guidance for this dialogue in its "Declaration on the Relationship of the Church to Non-Christian Religions," its "Declaration on Religious Freedom," and its "Dogmatic Constitution of the Church" (particularly No. 16).

2   The number of publications on the Japanese "new religions" has grown rapidly in recent years. Their relation to Buddhism is

discussed in W. Kohler, *Die Lotus-Lehre und die modernen Religionen in Japan* (Zurich, 1962). See also H. Neill McFarland, *The Rush Hour of the Gods, A Study of New Religious Movements in Japan* (New York and London, 1967), and H. Thomsen, *The New Religions of Japan* (Tokyo, 1963).

3   Cf. Heinrich Dumoulin, "Buddhismus im modernen Japan," in *id.,* ed., *Buddhismus der Gegenwart* (Freiburg, New York and London, 1970), pp. 127ff.; see also N. S. Brannen, *Sōka-Gakkai, Japan's Militant Buddhists* (Richmond, Va., 1968); and J. A. Dator, *Sōka-Gakkai, Builders of the Third Civilization* (Seattle and London, 1969).

4   On the quest for unity, present in all religions but not attainable by hastily glossing over differences, see R. Panikkar, *Religionen und die Religion* (Munich, 1965), p. 165: "If the adherents of all religions try in humility to climb the path to holiness, they do more for the unity of all confessions than can be done by all attempts to radically abolish all differences."

5   On the occasion of a discussion on the "encounter between Christianity and Buddhism" in Japan, the well-known Japanese Lutheran theologian, K. Kitamori, remarked that "if one looks back in retrospect, it is regrettable that the relationship between Buddhism and Christianity developed in parallel lines, or to put it more strongly, in an awareness of opposition. On the other hand, reduction of all teachings to one has led ultimately to syncretism. But neither syncretism nor parallelism offer, to my mind, the genuine solution." From *Asahi Shimbun,* 24 September 1967.

6   Among the wealth of the existing literature, on the difficult subject of the claims to absoluteness on the part of Christianity as well as of non-Christian religions, see above all Heinrich Fries, "Absolutheitsanspruch des Christentums," *Lexikon für Theologie und Kirche* I (Freiburg, Basel and Vienna, 1963), pp. 71-74, where an extensive bibliography is given. Fries particularly examines the use of the concept "absolute" (that is, not relative, unconditional, universally valid) and its development since the time of German idealism. Of older literature we may mention Ernst Troeltsch, *Die Absolutheit des Christentums und die Religionsgeschichte* (Tubingen, 1929). See also Joseph Ratzinger, "Das Problem der Absolu-

theit des christlichen Heilsweges," in W. Bold et al., editors, *Kirche in der ausserchristlichen Welt* (Regensburg, 1967). On the necessary distinction between the claims to absoluteness and exclusiveness in religions, see Elisabeth Gössmann, "Absolutheit oder Ausschliesslichkeit? Der Anspruch des Christentums und der Sinn der Mission," *Stimmen der Zeit,* vol. 187, no. 7 (1966), pp. 11-24.

7   Observations of well-known Japanese non-Christians on this subject are cited in H. Waldenfels, "Anmerkungen zum Gespräch der Christenheit mit der nichtchristlichen Welt," *Kirche in der ausserchristlichen Welt* (Regensburg, 1967), pp. 95-141. As the remark by the Japanese Buddhist clearly shows, many extensive and penetrating treatises by well-known theologians on the essential relations between non-Christians and Christians (e.g., Karl Rahner's writings on the "anonymous Christian") are not likely to promote the interreligious dialogue, as significant as they may be in other respects.

8   A typical, even classic example, is the meeting of the first Christian missionary in Japan, Francis Xavier, with a Zen Buddhist, the monk Ninshitsu; see Dumoulin, *A History of Zen Buddhism,* pp. 200ff.

9   The so-called "theology of religions" deals with the question, whether and to what extent non-Christian religions might be regarded as institutions which promote the salvation of mankind. Here we do not treat the question further, other than to assert our view that non-Christian religions definitely count among the positive and saving factors in the history of mankind. Jean Daniélou recognized the unique value of non-Christian religions as "advents" some time ago; cf. "Le problème théologique des religions non Chrétiennes" (*Archivo di filosofia,* 1956), pp. 214-216; *Der Gott der Heiden, der Juden und der Christen* (Mainz, 1957). From the wealth of the recent Catholic literature on this subject, may be mentioned the following: Karl Rahner, "Das Christentum und die nichtchristlichen Religionen" and "Weltgeschichte und Heilsgeschichte," *Schriften zur Theologie* V (Einsiedeln-Zurich-Cologne, 1964), pp. 136-158 and 115-136; "Die anonymen Christen," *Schriften zur Theologie* VI (1965), pp. 545-554; "Kirche, Kirchen

und Religionen," *Schriften zur Theologie* VIII (1967), pp. 355-373. Further: H. R. Schlette, "Die Religionen als Thema der Theologie," *Quaestiones disputatae* XXII (Freiburg, 1964); *Die Konfrontation mit den Religionen* (Cologne, 1964); *Colloquium salutis—Christen und Nichtchristen heute* (Cologne, 1965); also Heinrich Fries, "Das Christentum und die Religionen der Welt," in K. Forster, ed., *Das Christentum und die Weltreligionen* (Würzburg, 1967), pp. 13-37; G. Thils, *Propos et problèmes de la théologie des religions non Chrétiennes* (Tournai, 1966). The Protestant contributions to this topic are no less important; see, for example Paul Tillich, *Christianity and the Encounter of the World Religions* (New York–London, 1965); Ernst Benz, *Ideen zu einer Theologie der Religionsgeschichte* (Mainz, 1960); R. Slater, *Can Christians Learn from Other Religions?* (New York, 1963); Stephen Neill, *Christian Faith and Other Faiths* (London, 1965); C. J. Bleeker, *Christ in Modern Athens* (Leiden, 1965); G. Rosenkranz, *Der christliche Glaube angesichts der Weltreligionen* (Bern, 1966).

10   With increasing frequency, introductory courses on non-Christian religions are being included in the curricula for students of theology. The necessity of such courses seems beyond doubt. The Secretariat for the Dialogue with Non-Christian Religions has recently published a series of introductory booklets on this subject; on Buddhism, see the second volume entitled *Towards the Meeting with Buddhism* (Rome, 1970).

11   In the short paragraph characterizing the essential features of the individual non-Christian religions, the "Declaration on the Relation of the Church to Non-Christian Religions" sets forth their basic religious tenets and most important values and offers worthwhile references for the dialogue. Concerning the text of the Council document, see the commentary of Heinrich Dumoulin in: *Lexikon für Theologie und Kirche, Das Zweite Vatikanische Konzil, Kommentare, Teil II* (Freiburg, 1967), pp. 482-485. On the two ways of salvation by *jiriki* and *tariki,* see Heinrich Dumoulin, "Grace and Freedom in the Way of Salvation in Japanese Buddhism," in R. J. Zwi Werblowsky and C. J. Bleeker, ed., *Types of Redemption* (Leiden, 1970), pp. 98-104.

12   On the distinction between "structurally Christian" and "existentially Christian," see H. R. Schlette, *Colloquium Salutis-Christen und Nichtchristen heute* (Cologne, 1965), p. 83; also Elisabeth Gössmann, *op. cit.,* pp. 15-19. On structurally Christian phenomena, see also Gössmann's *Religiöse Herkunft—Profane Zukunft? Das Christentum in Japan* (Munich, 1965), pp. 9-22, 159-165.

13   On the political views of of Sōka-Gakkai, see the paragraph entitled "Politische Religion oder religiöse Politik?" in Dumoulin, "Buddhismus im modernen Japan," *op. cit.,* pp. 181-187.

14   *Ibid.,* p. 173.

15   This work was published in Japanese soon after the end of the Second World War. English translation: *Theology of the Pain of God* (Richmond, Va., 1965). For a Catholic assessment, see the review by P. Nemeshegyi in *The Japan Missionary Bulletin,* vol. XXI (April 1967), pp. 187-190.

16   Yagi, who studied in Göttingen under Ernst Käsemann, has recently become well known through his publications and especially through contemporary theological controversies. In the preface to his book on the emergence of New Testament categories, *Shinyaku seishō no seiritsu* (Tokyo, 1963), he tells of his experience with Christianity: "My sins pained me; I believed in the forgiveness of sins through the cross and I was newly born. I recognized life, which cannot be lived without the cross" (p. 3). He became interested in Buddhism in Germany. "From then on," he writes, "I began to understand Buddhism . . . I realized that essential points of agreement on the question of existence bind it to Christianity. These points are not theoretical, but rather existential" (p. 4). In the course of the book he takes up the theme of parallels between Christianity and Buddhism several times. Yagi follows Bultmann to a large degree in his understanding of the New Testament, and goes even further than Bultmann in some respects. Thus he became involved in a widely publicized controversy with the Japanese Barthian theologian Katsumi Takizawa. (Cf. the series of articles by John O. Barksdale, "Yagi and Takizawa—Bultmann vs. Barth

in Japan," *The Japan Missionary Bulletin,* vol. XXIV (1970), pp. 38-43, 93-100, 193-200, 215-222.)

17   See Dumoulin, *Östliche Meditation und christliche Mystik,* pp. 98-126. Michael Schmaus has written of the need for a more practical application of negative theology to Christian preaching in Japan: "Negative theology—according to which God is recognized more in nescience than in knowledge—should be a decisive element in fruitful dialogue." From "Einige Überlegungen zur christlichen Mission in Japan," *Asien—Tradition und Fortschritt: Festschrift für Horst Hammitzsch* (Wiesbaden, 1971), p. 539.

18   H. M. Enomiya-Lassalle has given a detailed account of his point of view in two books, *Zen—Way to Enlightenment* (New York, 1968) and *Zen-Buddhismus* (Cologne, 1966). Fr. Enomiya is a revered confrere of mine, who lived through the atomic catastrophe of Hiroshima, acquired Japanese nationality out of sympathy with the Japanese people, was made an honorary citizen of Hiroshima and built a Christian Zen hall near Tokyo. Fr. Enomiya's views on the mystical way are most clearly presented in his most recent book, *Meditation und Gotteserfahrung* (Cologne, 1972).

19   This Zen Master, Reirin Yamada, has meanwhile retired from the confusion of the Tokyo megapolis and the exhausting office of a university president (he was president of the Buddhist Komazawa University) into the mountain solitude and has become Abbot of the Zen monastery Eiheiji in Fukui Prefecture, which was founded by the famous Zen Master, Dōgen.

20   See Dumoulin, "Grace and Freedom in the Way of Salvation in Japanese Buddhism," *op. cit.*

21   On the relationship of the Kyoto school of philosophy to the metaphysics of Zen Buddhism, see the study of H. Waldenfels, "Absolute Nothingness, Preliminary Considerations on a Central Notion in the Philosophy of Nishida Kitaro and the Kyoto School," *op. cit.*

22   Hakuin describes the therapeutic methods in his work, "Yasen Kannan," English translation by R. D. M. Shaw and W. Schiffer, *Monumenta Nipponica,* vol. XIII (1957), pp. 101-127.

23   Thomas Merton has often mentioned that Buddhist compassion rests on "a basic and unclouded realism in . . . dealings with other people." Such compassion might well offer access to social and even political commitment. In fact, the Sōka-Gakkai emphasizes the significance of compassion (*jihi*) for political negotiation. Cf. "Buddhismus im modernen Japan," *op. cit.,* p. 186.

24   On the first conference in Oiso, see the author's complete report in *Concilium,* vol. III (November 1967), pp. 763-771. The Oiso conference adopted a resolution to hold such a meeting annually, and this resolution has been kept. At the sixth conference, held in August 1972, the conferees considered the possibility of including the general public in the discussions. It was apparent that the fruit of the first six conferences was a deep mutual trust and direction toward the essential problems of religion. More must be understood and undertaken, but all participants agreed their mutual efforts were relevant to the problem, and some professed they had been spiritually enriched by the conferences.

25   See note 7. Here we cannot delve further into the discussion inspired by Karl Rahner's theology of the "anonymous Christian." Michael Schmaus, in a new work on Christian dogmatics, suggests the concept of the "potential Christian"; see *Der Glaube der Kirche* I (Munich, 1969), pp. 128ff. Henri de Lubac distinguishes between the "anonymous Christian" and "anonymous Christianity" rejecting the latter, along with "implicit Christianity." See his *Geheimnis, aus dem wir leben* (Einsiedeln, 1967), pp. 149ff. Cf. Rahner's recent reply to de Lubac's objections: "Anonymes Christentum und Missionsauftrag der Kirche," *Schriften zur Theologie* IX (1970), pp. 498-515.

26   This is the *Nihon Shūkyō Remmei,* to which belong almost all religious bodies registered with the Ministry of Education, with the notable exception of Sōka-Gakkai.

27   During Japan's feudal period, religious practices in the strict sense were separated from morals and public life and relegated to the private sphere. This attitude was revealed in often contradictory ways in the attempts to create a new democratic popular morality after the termination of the Pacific War (1945). See Heinrich Dumoulin, "Die religiöse Geistigkeit des fernöstli-

chen Menschen im Gegenüber mit der westlichen Zivilisation," in R. Schwarz, ed., *Menschliche Existenz und moderne Welt* (Berlin, 1967), pp. 351ff.

28   The first was in 1968. In the following years common prayer meetings were held in the Catholic cathedral of Tokyo. In addition, the religious communities published a common appeal to the Japanese public pleading for prayer and constructive work for peace.

29   Cf. "Die Weltkonferenz für Religion und Frieden," *Aus dem Lande der aufgehenden Sonne,* vol. 80 (Winter 1970), pp. 15-17. There are, of course, "idealistic" Buddhists and "realistic" Protestants as well in Japan. Wherever political questions are raised, the limits of agreement and understanding come to light; and these questions are often the source of division within a particular religion itself.

30   Representatives of nine Asian countries participated in the conference. The Secretariat for Non-Christian Religions was also represented because, as the conference explicitly stated, the two secretariats pursue almost identical goals in Asia. In January 1971, the conference "Comité central du Conseil oecuménique des Eglises" was held in Addis Ababa. The question of interreligious dialogue was extensively discussed and its necessity for the work of Christian missions was emphasized. This conference also recognized the positive side of the secularization process and saw in that process a sign of human maturity.

31   For more on this subject, see *Buddhismus der Gegenwart.*

32   See, for example, J. Swyngedouw, "Secularization's Impact on Japanese Religion," *The Japan Missionary Bulletin,* vol. 25, No. 5 (June 1971), pp. 256-262, esp. p. 259.

33   Swyngedouw argues against those sociologists who "tend to dismiss Buddhism—and Eastern ways of thinking in general —as opposite to the trends of the time."*Ibid.,* p. 256.

34   A symposium of leading Buddhists on the theme "Buddhism and the Disclosure of Asia" (*Asia no kaihatsu to bukkyō*), held August 31, 1970, in Hakone, discussed the problems of modernization and the correlated tasks of Buddhism. On this occasion, H. Nakamura remarked that "although Asia's culture is Buddhis-

tic, Christianity has taken the lead in Asian social and political concerns." Such a remark clearly indicates the necessity for mutual cooperation between Buddhists and Christians in seeking the solution of economic problems in Asia.

35   On the first encounter between Buddhism and Christianity, see Henri de Lubac, *La Rencontre du Bouddhisme et de l'Occident* (Paris, 1952), pp. 9-32, and also his bibliography. On the influences in art see the standard reference work of A. Foucher, *L'art gréco-bouddhique du Gandhara* (Paris, 1905-1951). 4 vols.

36   On the Nestorians in China and the inscribed monument, see Charles Eliot, *Japanese Buddhism* (London, 1935), pp. 148ff. & 394ff. Eliot writes of friendly relations between Buddhists and Nestorians, but considers the thesis of a significant Nestorian influence on the development of Buddhism unfounded. In his view, "the Nestorian monument indicates not that Nestorianism influenced Buddhism but that it abandoned the doctrine of atonement . . . ," in as much as the inscription treats in some detail the life of Christ, but omits mention of the crucifixion. *Hinduism and Buddhism,* vol. III (London 1921, reprinted 1968), p. 165. See also de Lubac, op. cit., p. 35.

37   De Lubac discusses this question at length in Chapter 10 ("La question des influences externes") of his book, *Amida* (Paris 1955), pp. 226-249, where he debates with the two main exponents of the theory of Christian influence on Amidism: Yoshiro Saeki, *The Nestorian Documents and Relics in China* (Tokyo 1937), *The Nestorian Monument in China* (London, 1916), and Arthur Lloyd *The Creed of Half Japan* (London, 1911), and "Shinran and his Work," in *Studies in Shinshu Theology* (Tokyo, 1910). De Lubac holds that any Christian influence was at most belated (p. 232), and emphasizes that *"tout l'essentiel de la doctrine Amidiste est déjà contenu dans les soutras fondamentaux."* (p. 234). De Lubac concludes that Amidism *"est en continuité profonde avec le Bouddhisme primitif"* (p. 248), and quotes several authors in support of this view.

38   The two basic sutras of Amida-Buddhism are the longer (and older) version (*Amitābhavyūha*) and the shorter version of the *Sūkhavatīvyūha.* The Major Sutra of the Pure Land names the

Buddha *Amithābha,* "of infinite light"; the Minor Sutra names the Buddha *Amitāyus,* "of infinite life." The Major Sutra was translated into Chinese ten times, and the first translation occurred as early as 180 A.D. according to H. von Glasenapp in *Der Buddhismus* (Berlin and Zurich, 1936 and 1959). The Minor Sutra is contained in the Chinese translation by Kumārajīva (d. 413).

39   On Iranian influences on Buddhism see Kenneth K. S. Ch'en, *Buddhism in China* (New York, 1964), pp. 15f.

40   For this phase of the Buddhist-Christian encounter see the second chapter ("Les grands Voyageurs") of de Lubac, *La Rencontre du Bouddhisme et de l'Occident,* pp. 33-48. The Franciscan reports contain many complimentary remarks about the strict ascetic life of Buddhist monks. John of Monte Corvino, for example, finds "these monks [are] more rigorous and strict in observance than Latin monks" (p. 41); and John Marignolli, who came over China to Ceylon, was amazed by the barefoot, mendicant monks who ate only once a day and drank milk and water (p. 46). At the end of the second chapter, de Lubac stresses the altogether complimentary manner in which the Christian missionaries wrote of Buddhist monks (p. 48).

CHAPTER 3

Religious and
Existential Experience

Today the dialogue between Buddhism and Christianity
is well underway. This is all the more surprising when
we recall the seemingly radical differences between the
two religions and the failure of earlier attempts at dialogue. The changing general situation of the world with
urbanization and improved communications is certainly a significant factor in today's unusual readiness
for mutual understanding. Thus, one can view the interreligious dialogue at least partially as arising from the
present world situation. In addition, the new theological situation demands our attention. There has been a
profound progress in theological insight in our time,

and non-Christians have their share in this as well as Christians. It appears that our appreciation of man's religious condition has come to the point where the Christian dialogue with other religions can succeed. Before we consider some of the theological aspects of the dialogue with Buddhism, it would be well to contrast today's situation with the totally different theological circumstances of two previous encounters. In both instances, the dialogue ran aground from lack of the requisite theological attitude.

In Japan, the first encounters between Buddhists and Christians date to the beginnings of the Christian missions of modern times. Francis Xavier, the first Christian missionary to step on Japanese soil, landed in Kagoshima, a port city on Japan's southern island, Kyushu, and soon afterwards paid a visit to a Zen Buddhist temple. There, in a well-known episode, Xavier befriended the old abbot Ninshitsu[1]; their conversations are preserved in the missionary annals and serve both as a paradigm of noble humanity and an authentic inter-religious exchange. On the basis of his experiences, Xavier thought religious debates between Christian missionaries and Buddhist monks were possible. The records of disputes between the Portuguese Jesuit Cosme de Torres and Japanese Buddhist monks, mainly of the Zen school of Yamaguchi, have been handed down to us as well[2]; the questions were passionately argued, but no meeting-ground was found. The learned Father—well known for his outstanding scientific knowledge and talent—tried in vain to prove the existence of God by scholastic argumentation to the Japanese monks whom de Torres otherwise esteemed as highly intelligent. And the Buddhists inexorably repeated the difficult axioms of Mahayanistic philosophy and enthusiastically spoke of primordial Nothingness. These talks miscarried primarily because the Christian missionaries took the Buddhist teachings to be nihilistic and failed to recognize the mystical character of the Buddhists' negative formulations.

When 19th century European science discovered Buddhism, first in the Hīnayāna and then the Mahā-yāna form, the resulting encounter with Christianity appeared very different. In Europe, it was the Age of Enlightenment and Rationalism, a time when there came to be known lucrative new sources of information about the non-Christian religions. Literature on the relation of Buddhism and Christianity grew extensively, reporting similarities and differences and offering different value judgments, according to the viewpoint of the author. There was no lack of serious attempts to attain a real understanding. Yet, overall, the predominant study of comparative religion at the turn of the century was more able to reveal opposing views than to create channels of communication.[3] A sympathetic dialogue between the religions could not emerge because public discussion had precluded theology and personal spirituality. The new history of religions, to be sure, contributed much valuable material for research, but the theology and spirituality it lacked are indispensable for a true interreligious dialogue.

Religious Experience as the Basis of Dialogue

Thus, in terms of historical prerequisites, the possibility of a Christian-Buddhist dialogue seemed slight indeed even a few years ago. Insufficient information gave the educated public the false but widespread impression that Buddhism was irrevocably opposed to a Christianity which believed in God's revelation—that Buddhism was atheistic, pantheistic, or even nihilistic.

Now, for our part, we are not about to disclaim profound differences between the two religions. Nor do we see a Christian dialogue with Buddhism as a simple matter which promises immediate results and is well on its way to its often quite vaguely conceived goal. In the previous chapter, we tried to specify possible objectives—such as mutual learning, understanding, and cooperation for the welfare of mankind—and at the same time to guard against any melting-pot syncretism or false ecumenism. We expect no sudden, striking or revolutionary realization of these objectives. The most valuable results escape statistical formulation. They are interior and need time to grow and prosper. Under these circumstances, the significance of the theological dimension is clear. If the dialogue has begun quickly and already borne some fruit, then this initial success is due foremost to the novel theological approaches which pave ways to communication and more fruitful discussion.

The successful spiritual encounter between Zen Buddhists and Christians at the Oiso meeting encouraged the conviction that a genuine and profound dialogue of considerable dimension is at hand. To be sure, the stage for this encounter had been set for decades. True, the 16th century Jesuit missionaries considered "the people of deep meditations"—so they called the Zen Buddhists —as "those most opposed to God's law." But three or four centuries later their confreres were attracted most to Zen Buddhism and discovered in the Buddhist way of meditation spiritual values and characteristics related to Christianity.[4] Our previous considerations of Zen Buddhism centered on the specifically Eastern manner of meditation, on intuition, and on negative theology. These characteristics, present universally in Buddhism, are proving more and more to be of vital importance for the Buddhist-Christian dialogue.

The disputes of earlier times concentrated mainly on the problem of God. The missionaries were not able to comprehend how Buddhists could see the absence of a notion of God as an advantage of their religion; nor did they understand that the Buddhists considered the Christian notion of God as unacceptably anthropomorphic. At the conference in Oiso, of course, the question of God was present from the very beginning, and all of the contributions, whether by Buddhist, Protestant, or Catholic, centered on this true and ultimate reality, the omega point of all experience. To the Eastern mind, it is clear that deep religious experiences are mysterious and ineffable, but that at the same time the mystery of reality is visible to the truly enlightened person. More than any others among the Buddhists, the followers of the Zen discipline are attracted to the Christian mysticism, for example, of Meister Eckhart or John of the Cross. Usually, however, they do not realize that Christian theology underlies the experiences of these mystics, who are not religious outcasts but part of the Christian tradition. In Christianity, in addition to cataphatic or positive theology, there has been a tradition of apophatic or negative theology since Patristic times and even earlier. Both the positive and negative way are based on Holy Scripture and are familiar to such great Christian theologians as Gregory of Nyssa, Augustine and Thomas Aquinas. The divine being which has revealed itself to us is ineffable, beyond all predications and can equally be called non-existent as well as existent, since it is the plentitude of perfection and transcendental Nothingness.[5]

Buddhist religious experience is for the most part bound up with meditation, and it is always directed toward ultimate reality. Whether the Buddhist in practice meditates in the lotus posture, or speaks the holy name countless times before the Buddha statue, he

strives to turn inward and to break through the conscious ego to the unknown Other—the breakthrough
which brings him closer to the ultimate fulfillment of
his being. Having been taught in the Buddhist tradition,
he prefers to name the Other "Nothingness." I once met
an old worshipper of Amida who exclaimed, as if giving
away a secret, "But Amida is Emptiness"—and all the
time he spoke, he fingered his prayer cord and mur-
mured the holy name of the Buddha.[6] He inwardly
experienced the Buddha Amida as Emptiness. Yet,
Emptiness and Nothingness as experienced prove to be
of unimaginable vitality. They are the totality, boundless, the Buddha. The sacred Buddha is the reality
which transcends all objects, but which objects of the
cult can symbolize, for example, when the sutras are
recited or rituals performed before the Buddha. And
what does the Buddhist mean by the "Buddha"? Is his
meaning different from the Christian's who calls upon
"God"? The dialogue between Buddhists and Christians which begins at this point can lead to the discussion of essential theological questions.

Uncovering the theological background of religious
experience is vitally important for the dialogue precisely
because the ties between experience and basic religious
concepts are thereby exposed. The dialogue is not limited to personal experiences—rather, through access to
the other religions and to the essence of religion, it
grows in breadth and depth.

Existential Experience and the Truth of Suffering

Another approach significant for the Buddhist-Christian dialogue is through those existential anthropologi-

cal experiences which are prior to explicitly religious experience and whose importance has recently been rediscovered by modern theology.[7] When these experiences enter into the interreligious dialogue, the way is paved not for a dogmatic debate but for an understanding of the teachings and ideas of the various religions. Modern Christian theologians emphasize that the words of Scripture and the doctrines of revelation are first embedded in life-situations (*Sitz im Leben*) and are understood conceptually only when the believer experiences their existential import. Now Buddhism does not involve a revelation in the Christian sense of the word, but bases itself instead on Shākyamuni's experience of enlightenment. This experience, formulated by the first sermon of the Buddha at Benares, proves to be an existential experience open to the Absolute.[8] Thus it is not too far afield to say that Buddhism rests on existential experience, reaches far into man's transcendence, and is close to the Christian's in many ways. From this viewpoint, existential experience and the meaning behind religious teachings open more ways for discussion than the religious doctrines.

The fundamental Buddhist experience concerning human existence is expressed in the Truth of Suffering, the first of the so-called Four Noble Truths, which the Buddha preached after his enlightenment. What is meant is the experience of the radical plight and suffering of human existence. In Buddhism, this truth was seen in connection with the transience of all things, and was incorporated into all Buddhist schools without differentiation of the elements contained in it—suffering, pain, transience, finitude, and contingency—elements which Christian philosophy rightly differentiates. In Japanese Buddhism, the Truth of Suffering is expressed by the familiar word *mujo* ("unconstant"), and includes the content of the teachings as well as the feel of life.[9]

Apparently, the fundamental Buddhist experience of suffering is an existential experience which the Christian has as well, and which ultimately all humans share: the experience of the unsatisfactory condition of human life. In reality things are not as they should be, nor as we would like them to be. We need not concern ourselves here with the reasons for this existential fact; Buddhists are as little able as Christians to explain it rationally. Its importance for us is that this experienced fact evokes in man the demand for change, for liberation—in religious terms, for deliverance or redemption. Buddhism, because of its fundamental experience, is included among the religions of redemption, all of which in one manner or another experience man's need for liberation as part of his essence. Buddhism makes desire and ignorance primarily responsible for the plight of man during his life on earth. These two links in the twelve-part chain of causation do not suffice ultimately to explain suffering, in spite of their dynamic function in setting the causal process in motion. Yet, in terms of general human experience, they are easily recognized as two factors which darken human life. Buddhism has painted a rather gloomy picture of man's fate of suffering and (especially in the climate of India) has frequently drawn pessimistic conclusions from man's existential situation. Nevertheless, the fundamental Buddhist experience need not be understood as ultimately pessimistic. We note that the Buddha has in mind man's present dilemma, which is judged as grave by Christians as well (for example in Paul's Epistle to the Romans). Nevertheless, by virtue of the Buddhist's existential experience of suffering, we may profitably speak, with him, of the meaning, the character and the degree of justifiable human pessimism.

Conversion and Non-Ego

The Buddhist-Christian dialogue becomes more profound when we reach the point of considering the consequences which, for the Buddhist, follow from the plight of human existence. Here we encounter the two basic religious experiences which we Christians call conversion and faith. In Christianity, the experience of faith holds priority; in Buddhism, the lived experience of a breakthrough or conversion which touches the true self is more important. This breakthrough, exacting to the self, is grounded in the existential fact of suffering. It teaches us that, because man does not find himself in his authentic mode of existence, both his stance towards his worldly environment and, even more, his ego-consciousness are in dire need of a conversion.

The original Buddhist theory of the non-ego (Pāli: *anattā*), owing especially to the philosophical consequences drawn by the Hīnayāna Schools, has met with opposition in Western philosophy. The opposition is in part justified, but there is a kernel of truth for existential experience contained in the doctrine of the non-ego. I refer to the truth that man must undergo a conversion, a breakthrough or awakening, in order to become his true self and gain access to what is authentically real. Zen Buddhism names this conversion the "great death" (*taishi*)—the sole way by which man can enter true life.[10] Life-and-death is a favorite theme of Zen-Buddhists, and they like to articulate this theme in the dialogue with Christians because here the beliefs of the two are contiguous. They are familiar with the paradoxical words of our Lord, "lose your life, in order to gain it," and with the Pauline theology: "die, so that you may live"; and they are fascinated by the words of Paul, "No longer do I live, Christ lives in me." Buddhists understand these passages in Scripture to be testimonies that this phenomenal, temporary ego must die so that one may attain authentic life.

Teilhard de Chardin has expressed in modern language the fundamental human experience of dying in order to live. In an early memorandum (1919) to his friend, Auguste Valensin, he wrote that "the consummation of the world follows only through a 'death,' a reversal, through a surge from below and, as it were, through a depersonalization of the monads."[11] And in his famous "Mass on the World," Teilhard prays, "O Lord, the World can ultimately reach you only through a kind of conversion, excentrization . . ." The motif of conversion, release, renunciation, of death for resurrection, has a well-known place in Christian spirituality and mysticism. Here we doubtlessly have to do with a basic experience of religious existence which leads to a realm shared in common by Buddhists and Christians.

The Christian tends to look for moral considerations in the Buddhist teaching of the non-ego. For no genuine experience of conversion can neglect questions of morality, and the Christian has been brought up to appreciate such questions. However, an over-emphasis on the moral can misstate the hierarchy of values given in the gospel. "Seek first the kingdom of God!" Yet moral considerations, as well, can be a part of what is laid out for anyone earnestly seeking the way.[12]

Over and above the question of morality, the Buddhist teaching of the non-ego must be considered as a whole, with all of its consequences for practical life. The adoption of the Buddhist ideal—whether in experiencing enlightenment, in taking up the way of the Bodhisattva, or in simply living everyday life—signifies in every case the indwelling of the basic Buddhist virtue of compassion (Sanskrit: *maitrī* and *karunā;* Japanese: *jihi*). Goodness emanates from the Buddhist who has perfectly attained the state of non-ego. And if goodness is the whole of moral life, then it is indeed misleading to characterize the Buddhist way as one "beyond good and evil," as is often done.[13] In the writings of Buddhist masters, including those from the Zen school, the disciples are persistently exhorted to lead a moral life. Just as the Zen master Hakuin continually admonished the people of the village near his poor country temple to lead a good life, so contemporary Zen masters instruct their followers who have attained enlightenment in the arts of moral living and character formation. Finally, Buddhists and Christians agree that nothing deters man from good as much as his clinging greedily to his ego.

Faith and Deliverance

Faith, as a necessary attitude and a lived experience, is amply witnessed in Buddhist scriptures—in the Pāli canon of ancient Buddhism, in the sutras and shastras of the Mahāyāna school, and in the religious writings of the other schools as well. But in spite of the wealth of material, one is hard put to understand Buddhist faith correctly. This faith is not a belief in dogma, not even in rationally known truths, and it is not primarily a belief in a person. These elements familiar to the

Westerner through the Christian concept of faith, are for the most part lacking in Buddhism.

The concept of revelation, so closely connected to the Christian notion of faith, is not characteristic of Buddhism—for the evident reason that revelation in the Christian sense is not possible without belief in a personal God. Nevertheless, religious elements based on divine revelation in Christianity also appear in Buddhism in a different, though related context and form. Buddhism, for example, recognizes a religious authority which ultimately derives from the Buddha's experience of enlightenment. Shākyamuni's first preaching, the famous sermon of Benares, received its power of authority from the fact of his enlightenment. To be sure, this sermon does not proclaim new truths. Rather, the disciple awakened by the Buddha's preaching is exhorted to find truth through his own experience. Buddhism does not subscribe to the idea that truth is communicated by hearing the revealed word. But it does recognize holy scriptures which are thought by the faithful to contain the word of the Buddha and to command great authority. The Buddhist canon, unlike Christian Scriptures, is not regarded as a source of revelation. Rather its authority is based on Shākyamuni's experience of enlightenment. In the course of this section, we shall deal more thoroughly with the significance of the Buddhist canon for its believers.

In order to grasp the essence of Buddhist faith, one would do well to consider the general human phenomenon of faith as primordial trust which promises man the ultimate fulfillment of his nature. In Buddhism, faith is directed to the final deliverance. To the extent that it promises man liberation from suffering, it is an expression of the fundamental Buddhist experience of the radical plight of human existence. Understood in this way, the faith of the Buddhist is necessarily linked to hope, specifically the hope of reaching the ultimate, felicitous and liberating goal of Nirvāna or the highest enlightenment.

The Buddhist experiences the salvation promised him as a "grace" in the broad sense of that word. He sees the final attainment of salvation as the fruit of a long process of growth conditioned by many things outside of his own decisions and attempts. Thus his salvation is a gift which delights him and obliges him to be grateful. The Buddhist scriptures often mention thanksgiving for the special privilege of being admitted to the Buddhist path of salvation. Emphasized as worthy of thanks above all is the privilege of hearing Buddha's teaching and, before hearing, the privilege of having been born a man who is able to hear.[14]

The basic pronouncements on faith in the Pāli canon connect faith with deliverance—"By faith you shall be free and go beyond the realm of death" (Suttanipāta II, 46), and "By faith the flood is crossed" (II, 184).[15] The flood refers to this transitory, pain-ridden world of human existence, and the crossing to the "other shore" means deliverance. The comparison between following the Buddhist path of salvation and crossing a stream is especially popular in early Buddhism. Through faith, man steps into the stream; faith represents the first indispensable entry into the Buddha-*Dharma*. "One awakens faith when entering into the great sea of the Buddha-*Dharma;* one uses knowledge to cross it. The true justice is faith. If a man's mind is full of true faith, he can easily enter into the Buddha-*Dharma;* without faith a man cannot enter into the Buddha-*Dharma*." [16] Similarly, in the Avatamsaka-Sutra, faith is called the "ground underlying the way and the mother of merits." The text continues: "Faith lets all good *dharmas* grow and scatters all doubts; it displays and opens the highest way." [17]

The faith which opens entrance to the *Dharma* and provides deliverance is awakened as soon as man turns to the path of salvation and experiences the first truth of the radical plight and suffering of all living creatures. This experience is by no means completely negative. The Buddhist does not submerge himself hopelessly in pain and suffering, but rather, during his contemplation of the first of the Four Noble Truths, takes his first step on the path of salvation. The other three truths, of the origination, the cessation and the way to the cessation of suffering, are inseparably linked to the first truth which simply states the fact of suffering. Shākyamuni understood the connection between these Four Holy Truths in the moment of the great experience that made him the Buddha. Through that experience, he became the one perfectly enlightened and perfectly liberated. Through faith, the disciple follows the Buddha who "has gone thus" (*tathā-gata*) in his path of salvation, and trusts that he will reach the other shore. One can view this belief in final salvation as the center of the Buddhist's experience of faith.

Faith is present in many forms in the religion of the Buddha, but the basic moment of belief in salvation appears in all. Here we may consider a passage which is fundamental for the understanding of Buddhist faith; it occurs with modifications several times in the Pāli canon. The follower of the Buddha is admonished to take refuge in the "three jewels": the Buddha, the *Dharma* (the teaching), and the *Sangha* (the community).

If a monk thinks and knows that these [aforementioned vices] are defilements of the mind and gets rid of them, he becomes possessed of unwavering confidence in the Buddha and thinks: "Thus indeed is he the Lord, Arahant, perfect Buddha, endowed with knowledge and right conduct, wellfarer, knower of the worlds, incomparable charioteer of men to be tamed, teacher of *devas* and mankind, a Buddha, a Lord." And he becomes possessed of unwavering confidence in *Dhamma* and thinks: '*Dhamma* is well taught by the Lord; it is thoroughly seen here and now; it is timeless, inviting all to come and see, leading onwards (to *Nibbāna*), to be understood by the wise each for himself.' And he becomes possessed of unwavering confidence in the Order and thinks: 'The Lord's Order of disciples is of good conduct, upright, of wise conduct, of dutiful conduct . . . This Order of the Lord's disciples is worthy of alms, hospitality, offerings and reverence; it is a matchless field of merit for the world.[18]

This text lays the foundation for the Buddhist scriptural teachings on faith. In the *Abhidharmakosha,* somewhat like a *Summa* of the Theravāda teachings, the series of existential factors which promote salvation and effect good karma begins with faith. To faith is ascribed a purifying function: "Faith cleanses the spirit." The commentary of Yasomitra explains that the spirit stained by passions is purified by the bond with the *Dharma* of faith, much as water in contact with a purifying gem becomes pure. Faith, as the commentator continues, principally contains the attitude of mind signified by the three jewels, and is ultimately traced back to the three recourses to the Buddha, the *Dharma* and the *Sangha.*[19] And according to the idealistic Vijñānavāda school, the three jewels constitute a principal content of faith. This school also recognizes the purifying function of faith, but develops the teaching on faith particularly in the psychological direction—faith awakens patience, joy and hope.[20]

The "Treatise on the Awakening of Faith in Mahā-yāna," as its title suggests, treats faith in detail. It names four kinds of faith. First is faith in the foundation, i.e. the Absolute, which it considers joyfully. Next are the three kinds of faith whose subject matter are the three jewels. An exhortation to ascetic exercises is added to the discussion of the various forms of faith. This clearly expresses the connection between faith and practice which Mahāyāna Buddhism considers so important.[21]

Refuge in the three jewels is all the more important when it is accorded an outstanding place in the cult. Disciples of the Buddha from all schools daily renew their refuge in the jewels. And many expressions of Buddhist faith can be considered reflections of the three jewels.

Refuge in the Buddha evolves into worship of the Buddha, which itself takes on various forms. First is the worship of the historical Buddha. Simultaneous with the historical Shākyamuni's elevation to the super-human realm was the intensification of the disciples' believing trust in the person of the Buddha. The titles of the Buddha, which in the text of the Pāli canon quoted above describe his super-human size and dignity worthy of veneration, are testimony of the faith of those disciples who handed on this representation of Buddha. The monuments passed down to us from pre-Christian times, especially the beautiful stupas of Sānchī and Bhā-rhut, are evidence that the worship of the Buddha was a vital part of the religious practice of Buddhism from its very beginnings.[22] The Buddha-devotees chiseled in stone there are shown worshipping the Lord Buddha, the perfected one who walked the path of salvation to its end and thus attained liberation and enlightenment. This Buddha above all serves as the figurehead of the savior in the mind of his faithful.

Mahāyāna Buddhism developed Buddhology further. The world of the Buddha which is disclosed to the followers of the Mahāyāna faith comprises the three bodies of the Buddha: the apparitional body (*nirmāna-kāya*), the body of bliss or enjoyment (*sambhoga-kāya*), and the cosmic body of the *Dharma* (*dharma-kāya*), as well as countless Buddhas and Bodhisattvas, each of which has a special function in assisting the disciple of the Buddha to progress along the path of salvation. Devotees of Mahāyāna faithfully worship the other appearances of the Buddha-world in the same way as they worship the historical Buddha, Shākyamuni. In the Mahāyāna sutras, the Lankāvatāra Sutra and the Brahmajāla Sutra, for example, ten ways of belief are named, reflecting the wealth of widespread devotion to the Buddha.

Faith and devotion characterize the entirety of Mahāyāna Buddhism. Of special significance in this respect is the worship of Amitābha (Japanese *Amida*), which is also called the "Buddhism of faith." In Japan, the most active form of this Buddhism is the form organized in the Pure Land Sects. Amitābha, the Buddha of infinite light and immeasurable life, has evoked more than any other Buddha the faithful trust of numerous worshippers. His throne is in the Western Paradise and his figure is of immense plenitude. But his faithful rely above all on his saving vows which assure even weak and sinful man final salvation. Nature and the effects of faith have been deeply pondered in the Pure Land Sects, and a kind of theology of faith has grown up. This theology has its summit in the writings of the Japanese Patriarch Shinran. His "Booklet on Regret over the Deviations from Faith," compiled posthumously by his disciple Yuiembō, teaches that faith "which is given by the Buddha" is alone effective in gaining salvation.[23]

Faith as it is shown in the various forms of Buddha veneration to some extent approximates the Christian understanding of faith. On the psychological side, there is probably no essential difference between the attitude of faith expressed in devotion to the Buddha and the popular Christian faith in God. Yet one must not overlook the provisional or temporary character of Buddhist faith. One acquires salvation in attaining Nirvāna or enlightenment, in the absolute realm which the Buddha and all of his disciples considered unspeakable—no matter how their forms of belief might otherwise differ. Faith, notwithstanding its primary importance in Buddhism, remains one mediating factor among others; it is not considered the cause of salvation.

The same may be said of the Buddhist expressions of faith which are sparked by the *Dharma.* The *Dharma* first of all signifies the teaching, that is, the word of the Buddha, which is passed down from generation to generation in the scriptural canon. The Buddhist approaches the words of his scriptures with belief; "he gives ear and hears *Dharma* and tests the things he has borne in mind, and they please him."[24] There is no lack of moving examples of reverence for the scriptures in the history of Buddhism. Even today, devoutly copying down a sutra counts as a meritorious work.[25] The "Bible of stone" in the precincts of the Kuthodaw temple of Mandalay in Burma represents a unique testimony to veneration of the word of Buddha in the scriptures. It consists of 729 stone tablets, each encircled by a small pagoda; chiseled into these in the entire Pāli canon. (All pagodas symbolize the Buddha. At Kuthodaw the smaller pagodas are arranged around one great stone pagoda.) The most ancient block-print of the canon representing both Hīnayāna and Mahāyāna Buddhism gives a similar impression of the sacred character of the scriptures. It is preserved on 81,000 wood-block tablets in two buildings of the temple Haeinsa in Korea.

To be sure, the teachings of the Buddha, like representations of him, serve no more than a mediating purpose in Buddhism. As the orthodox Zen Buddhist school dramatizes by word and gesture, all teachings are in essence unsatisfactory, even worthless. Teachings are no more than indications of the timelessly true accommodated to a different milieu.

Dharma, in addition to meaning "teaching," has taken on other significations in Buddhism. In Mahāyāna Buddhism, *Dharma* or the Principle of Being, is synonymous with the Buddha in his universal form. Along the lines of monistic philosophy, the *Dharma*-body of Buddha is conceived as present in all things and identical with all things. Linked to this conception is the teaching on universal Buddha-nature or on Buddha-mind, which facilitates a kind of faith particularly at work in meditation. The person meditating is instructed to awaken his belief in his own Buddha-nature; for Buddha-nature is the foundation not only of the universe but of the self as well. The extent to which this belief can be considered an authentic attitude of faith depends on the kind and degree of transcendence which is ascribed to Buddha-nature. Admittedly, at this point philosophical speculation can only too easily take over and disparage religious faith in Buddhism.

It is significant that the *Sangha,* the community, also serves a mediating function in the Buddhist experience of faith. Indeed, the Buddhist religion from its beginnings takes form in communities or brotherhoods of monks. The Buddha gathered disciples around himself, let them partake in his own experience, and encouraged them to strive earnestly for salvation. We know little about the early organization of the Buddhist community, but reports of the first Buddhist councils indicate that the institutional side of Buddhism was strongly developed after the Buddha's death. From that time on, the disciples of the Buddha were thoroughly convinced that they could best attain salvation in community. Theravāda Buddhist monasteries probably approximate the organization of the early communities of monks. And community spirit remained important in Mahā-yāna Buddhism as well, in spite of organizational changes throughout its history.

It is true that Mahāyāna Buddhism abandoned the monastic ideal to a large extent. Nevertheless the concept was preserved in the various schools, the monasteries and the traditions derived from them. The community played an important role in the mediation of the decisive experiences of faith. The Buddhist cult in Mahāyāna is closely linked with the community. Many Buddhists prefer the temple and the meditation hall as the locus of their religious experiences, and this holds for declared lay Buddhism in the new religions of Buddhist lineage as well as in Buddhism itself. These new religions have in fact developed a particularly strong community life. When they espouse a return to original Buddhism and in their cult recite the formula of the refuge in the three jewels, it is evident that they especially have recourse to the third jewel, the community. At the present time, there is not yet a theology of the community in Buddhism. But the community counts as one mediating factor of salvation among others and thereby assumes its place in the practice of the Buddhist religion.

Since Christianity is essentially a religion of faith, Christians will pay special attention to the expressions of faith within Buddhism. And surely the rich faith of Buddhism offers an important point of departure for the mutual exchange of ideas and experiences. But again we must not overlook the fact that, in Buddhism, every manner of belief and way of faith is considered mediatory and provisional. The Buddhist believer is committed to transcend every mediation and form, and not to cling to anything temporary. The true matter at hand, the attainment of liberation, lies beyond all means. One might ponder here, whether and in what sense one can affirm a similar statement concerning the experience of faith in Christianity.

In addition, faith is an important theme in the inter-religious dialogue because the forms of Buddhist faith make up the greater part of the Buddhist's everyday religious practice. They are ultimately derived from a primeval religious experience of man which, as we saw earlier in this chapter, is immediately linked to the experience of suffering. Just as the Buddhist in his heart is aware of the human condition, so he is cognizant of the possible liberation from suffering. Trusting in the depths of his soul, the believer reaches beyond his own suffering for a comprehensive, sheltering, guiding power that makes itself known to him in many ways. He transcends the boundaries of his ego and, as one Buddhist put it, feels "drawn by a pure and sublime power"[26] which promises him the ultimate realization of his being. The existential experience underlying all human faith—the experience that all things in the end have purpose and aid in salvation—can be seen to be at work in the many versions of faith in Buddhism as well.

The Experience of Transcendence

Man's deepest existential experiences disclose a transcendent reality. We have already touched upon this point several times. Undoubtedly there is a transcendent dimension in the religious essence of Buddhism; it has often been recognized by Buddhist and non-Buddhist alike. The Buddhist religion is unique, however, in that usually it does not directly aim for transcendent reality; rather, the transcendent dimension remains, as it were, in the background. It has been noted that there is no single religious notion in Buddhism which exactly corresponds to the absolute reality Christians call God. Impersonal ideas such as Nirvāna or *Dharma*, or even the symbols and manners of appearance of the Buddha, can possess an absolute value in the religious life of the Buddhist. In the case of a theistic religion, the entire idea of transcendence may be subsumed under the notion of a personal God. Buddhism, however, must be carefully investigated for those experiences which direct one to transcendent reality. The complexity of the matter demands a prudent approach.

Not long ago, Buddhism, particularly in its early forms, was considered by Westerners as "atheism." Today's scholars of religion are more circumspect in this matter,[27] first of all because they realize that the later forms of Buddhism, permeated with theistic elements (especially Mahāyāna Buddhism), cannot be separated from their origins. The element of transcendence, apparent in many forms in Mahāyāna, is never completely excluded in the religion of the Buddha. Still, transcendence in Buddhism is not grasped at first sight, but requires a closer look. Buddhists frequently feel a more or less strong aversion to the idea of God, according to the particular lineage they belong to. They are not inclined to impose a name upon the absolute, transcendent reality, although their religious life is permeated with a striving for transcendence. The spiritual oscillation evident here is characteristic of all Buddhism. The silence of the Buddha with respect to "metaphysical questions" began this attitude, and it has prevailed throughout the millennia of Buddhist history.

Buddhists are often content with a kind of "relative transcendence," one which goes beyond this empirical and relative world, but which does not in itself comprise the absolute, definitive, eternal realm. Relative transcendence is experienced, for example, when one compares the boundless universe with the finite, empirical world it transcends. Or, along the lines of depth-psychology, relative transcendence may be experienced in the breakthrough of the empirical ego to the reality of the self transcending the ego.[28] In both cases, the transcendence experienced, despite its relativity, can serve as the basis of religious attitudes. One might dwell in this relative stage for a long time before some crisis or deep sense of disillusionment brought him to a realization of absolute transcendence.

In its various schools, Buddhism proffers, for deliverance from the human condition of suffering, ways of liberation which are intended to thrust the individual into the experience of authentic transcendence.[29] Above and beyond this limited human existence, one can intuit an "Other," a "presence," a "positive and final end" which releases one from everything provisional and temporary. As an ancient text in the Pāli canon puts it, "There is, monks, an unborn, not become, not made, and were it not, monks, for this unborn, not become, not made, uncompounded, no escape could be shown here for what is born, has become, is made, is compounded."[30] This which is unconditioned is called 'Nirvāna' in original Buddhism and in Theravāda Buddhism, but on no account can it be understood as nihilistic. Hajime Nakamura emphasizes that, "Contrary to the prevalent Western opinion about Nirvāna, the craving for extinction in the sense of annihilation or non-existence (*vibhava-tanhā*) was expressly repudiated by the Buddha. Buddists search not for mere cessation, but for the eternal and the immortal."[31]

The transcendent dimension of Buddhist experience has stimulated a great variety of theoretical doctrine in Buddhology with regard to the figure of the Buddha. Admittedly, particular interpretations of Buddhism can underplay the role of the Buddha's historical appearance so much that it hardly seems essential to the Buddhist religion. Nevertheless, in the lived Buddhism of all schools, the Buddha has always stood at the center of the religion. The perspectives on his figure are so numerous and varied that only with difficulty can they be comprehended in a unified theology. It is hardly even possible to specify a single religious category which would contain the figure of the Buddha. At least, the Western study of comparative religion can determine no one fixed category for the purpose. The Buddha seems to constitute a special category particular to the East, one open to transcendence in the complexity of its implications.

Two particular directions point to transcendence in the religious experience of Buddhists. First is the tendency to elevate the Buddha-figure to a superhuman sphere transcending natural forces; second is the design to see the Buddha as the "other power" assisting man toward deliverance.[32]

The elevation of the historical Shākyamuni to the superhuman realm, which began soon after he entered Nirvāna, left his body as well as his mind imbued with extraordinary qualities and characteristics, including the power to work miracles. This exaltation of Shākyamuni is due to the enlightenment by which he gained Buddhahood. He is to be placed in the category of the Buddha, the transcendent significance of which is illustrated by the stories of Shākyamuni's previous existence. The mythical *Jātaka* stories, in the best interpretation of them, expound the meaning of Buddhahood. Not only do they extol the higher virtues associated with Buddhahood, above all the basic Buddhist virtue of selfless compassion with all living beings; but they also suggest a providence which guides the destiny and appearance of the historical Buddha Shākyamuni as well as of all Buddhas to come. The liberal use of *Jātaka* motifs in early Buddhist art demonstrates the great significance of these stories for religious life in ancient Buddhism. On the basis of historical sources, it is impossible to ascertain whether Buddhist monks opposed the introduction of mythical elements into their religion. In any case, even in the rational teaching of the Pāli canon, the Buddha is represented distinct from his disciples and followers as a unique figure belonging to a special category. Transcending all limitations, the Buddha is for his faithful the object of awe and veneration and an absolute ideal.

The history of religion has often taken the superhuman dimension of the Buddhas and Bodhisattvas of Mahāyāna Buddhism to be a kind of polytheism. Yet these figures also belong to the unique Buddha category; they are Buddhas by virtue of their enlightenment, and they are clearly distinguished from such celestial beings as the *devas* or *apsaras*. In addition, Mahāyāna Buddhism also speaks of universal Buddhas. Like the cosmic Buddha Vairocana of the Avatamsaka Sutras, or the eternal Buddha who reveals himself at the apex of the Lotus Sutra and whose temporal embodiment is Shākyamuni,[33] these universal figures in all their attributes are meant to represent nothing other than the transcendence and absolute character of the Buddha.

In the Mahāyāna sutras we find a world of symbols, but we must not forget that these symbols originated in religious experiences which, in the language of the symbols themselves, prove to be experiences of transcendence. Born from experience, the symbols of transcendence are able to lead one back to experience.

Buddhist art has represented the transcendent dimension of the Buddha-experience in two main forms. First are the colossal statues of the Buddha, such as we find in Sokkuram, Korea, and in Nara and Kamakura, Japan. The immense size of such statues in some way points to absolute quantity. One is led from sensual impressions of the height and sublimity of these statues to that which transcends all sense-impressions. Further, Buddhist art favors the multiplication of Buddha-figures. This motif goes back to the so-called legend of the "Great Miracle of Srāvastī," in which Shākyamuni, sitting on a lotus flower, duplicates his figure countless times in all directions. Early Buddhist art often depicted this particular marvel.[34] Those who are conversant with Buddhist art in Asia know that the Buddha almost everywhere is widely represented. One is given a strong sense of transcendence, for example, by the number of mighty heads of the Buddha in the ruins of the temple Bayon in Angkor thom, Cambodia. Fifty-two Buddha heads peer out in all directions and, as it were, give the Bodhisattva Avalokiteshvara (who there is regarded as the "Lord of the Universe" and the highest Buddha) universal presence. The countless Buddha-figures of Borobudur, Java, transplant the pilgrim climbing up through the stone terraces into a transcendent Buddha-world, which terminates only at the highest stupa in Emptiness, the most profound symbol of transcendence. He who freely enters into the world of Buddhist art cannot help but experience therein the language of transcendence.

No less important for the religious life of Buddhists is the other gate to transcendence in which the Buddha is experienced as the helpful "other power" who assists the erring man on his path to salvation. This mode of experiencing the transcendent, like the mode depicted in the exalted Buddha-figure, is encountered throughout Buddhism, nourished by the scriptural canon, and is expressed in manifold ways in the works of art. This is not the place to trace its history from the days of Shākyamuni to the present. Here we must confine ourselves to mentioning two typical figures from later Buddhism especially relevant to religious life in East Asia.

First is the Bodhisattva Avalokiteshvara (Chinese: *Kuan Yin,* Japanese: *Kannon*), the most popular embodiment of the Mahāyāna ideal of Bodhisattva. Although the Chinese thought of Kuan Yin as feminine and, inspired by the East Asian folk religion, transformed her into a mother-goddess, nevertheless Kuan Yin or Kannon has remained a figure of the transcending Bodhisattva who commanded veneration for her compassion as well as for her wisdom. Whenever religious consciousness has elevated itself above merely popular belief, the Bodhisattva symbolizes the assisting participation of the supermundane world of the Buddha. In Japan, in addition to Kannon, several other Bodhisattvas enjoy considerable veneration—such as Manjusri (Japanese: *Monju*), the Bodhisattva of wisdom whose cult is profoundly religious.

The theological implications of the transcendent experience which seeks the "Other" have been most strongly felt in the religion of the Buddha Amitābha. The phenomenological similarity between this experi-

ence of transcendence and its Christian counterpart is
striking. Nevertheless, an immediate dependence of one
on the other need not be assumed—as we emphasized
earlier. And though the importance of the figure of
Buddha in Amidism suggests a monotheism, it must be
remembered that the basic teachings of monistic Mahāyāna philosophy are also maintained in the Amida faith.
Transcendence is chiefly experienced in connection
with deliverance, as it is in all forms of Buddhism.
However it may be represented, the "Other" is the
power which liberates and redeems. Amida Buddhism
terms it simply "the other power" (Japanese: *tariki*),
and charges it with the notion of the "completely other"
that in dialectical theology gives expression to the absolute transcendence of the divine being. The Amida disciple seeks the Other, the eternal One who transcends
and saves, and recognizes the reality of the Other in the
figure of the Buddha Amida. As the so-called *raigo*
paintings illustrate, it is Amida, glorious in the midst
of his heavenly hosts, who descends to meet the devout
disciple, his hand clutching the prayer-beads, in the
hour of death.

Faith in the "other power" is not confined to Amidism, but is alive in other Buddhist schools as well.
Modern Buddhists interpret the quest for the "other
power," in the existential sense, as an experience of
transcendence.[35]

Can we go a step further and understand the experience of transcendence in Buddhism in a *personal* sense?
Here the Christian-Buddhist dialogue has reached a
plateau, and circumspection is in order. Clearly the
concept of person is in need of clarification. It is not
difficult to point out personalistic attitudes in Buddhism, indeed, in all of its schools. In Amidism, the
figure of Amida personifies the light and the warmth

which inspire trusting surrender to the Buddha. Elsewhere I have noted how Zen disciples, during their long and difficult exercises, often spontaneously express a personal devotion.[36] It has frequently been noted that personal acts are fully present in the new religions which are connected with Nichiren Buddhism. And there are ample indications of personal religiosity in the popular forms of Theravāda Buddhism.

Such facts raise the question of deeper relations between the apersonal cosmic and the personal within the Buddhist religion. We shall take up this question in the next chapter, which is concerned with Buddhist mysticism. There we will have occasion to touch once more upon the *theologia negativa* which we considered before in connection with religious experience in Buddhism. Wherever the Absolute is experienced as transcendent Nothingness, the negative formulation most clearly expresses absolute transcendence. Buddhist mysticism, like all mysticism, testifies to the transcendent dimension of man's religious experience. In the last chapter we shall attempt to clarify the relation between transcendent, ultimate reality and the personal.

The review of spiritual and existential experiences undertaken in this chapter opens up new possibilities for dialogue. By disclosing the depths of human spirituality, we have reconsidered previous positions and what have been considered fixed oppositions: optimism and pessimism, theism and atheism. We have thus expanded the horizon of understanding, barred for so long by scientific rationalism, especially in the West. The newly gained perspectives are truly theological, inspired and guided by the Spirit. Genuine encounter takes place without confusing differences. We do not close our eyes to differences, but rather pay them all the more attention, for it is precisely such differences that can teach us. Thus, through mutual understanding and learning, the dialogue goes on; and no matter what its particular form, it bears good things under the guidance of the Divine Word (*theo-logos*).

Notes

1   Related from the letters of Francis Xavier in Dumoulin, *A History of Zen Buddhism,* p. 199ff.; see the further details and literature quoted there on the encounter between Zen Buddhism and Christianity during the time of the early Christian missions to Japan.

2   See the source materials collated by G. Schurhammer, *Die Disputationen des P. Cosme de Torres mit den Buddhisten in Yamaguchi im Jahre 1551* (Tokyo, 1929).

3   The important Japanese Buddhist scholar Masaharu Anesaki certainly deserves mention in this connection, for he represents one of the very few exceptions to the rule. In his article, "How Christianity Appeals to a Japanese Buddhist" in the *Hibbert Journal,* vol. IV, no. 1 (1905), he writes that "A time will come when all the world will accept the Christian religion, but this will never abolish the difference of tastes and modes of expression . . . Buddhists will never lose their spirit of toleration. There may grow in Japan a form of Christianity without Pope and without Holy Synod, but Buddhism will nevertheless hold its footing therein for ever. In short, we Buddhists are ready to accept Christianity; nay, more, our faith in Buddha is faith in Christ. We see Christ because we see Buddha." This text is noteworthy because, in spite of a formulation unacceptable to us today, its intent is not far from insights which are gleaned in today's interreligious dialogue.

4   Father H. M. Enomiya-Lasalle made a Zen retreat (*sesshin*) in the temple of Tsuwano, in southern Japan, as early as the winter of 1942—exactly twenty years before the Second Vatican Council.

The next year saw publication of my first work on Zen, the translation of a Chinese Zen text: Heinrich Dumoulin, *The Development of Chinese Zen after the Sixth Patriarch in the Light of Mumonkan,* later translated from the German by R. F. Sasaki (New York, 1953).

5   Many recent theological works make a point of the significance of Christian negative theology. Of the numerous articles and talks by Karl Rahner, in which he speaks of the "ineffable mystery of God," we can mention here only his contribution "Geheimnis II, Theologisch," to the *Handbuch theologischer Grundbegriffe,* vol. I, H. Fries, ed. (Munich, 1962), pp. 447-452. In my book *Östliche Meditation und christliche Mystik,* pp. 98-124, I have collated several testimonies of Eastern and Western negative theology. In this regard, see also the chapter "Das schweigende Geheimnis Gottes" by M. Heinrichs in *Katholische Theologie und asiatisches Denken* (Mainz, 1963), pp. 104-140.

6   On the meditative character of the invocation of the name of the Buddha, see the author's *Östliche Meditation und christliche Mystik,* pp. 204-208. There the Abbess of a Vietnamese convent elucidates the stages of meditative invocation, whereby Amida is ultimately conceived of as Nothingness.

7   Out of fear that the emphasis on experience might reduce the motives of faith to the realm of the purely subjective and irrational, such emphasis was long held suspect by Catholic theology. Today theology is taking a fresh look at existential and historical experience. See for example W. Kasper, "Möglichkeiten der Gotteserfahrung heute," in *Geist und Leben,* vol. 42 (1969), pp. 329-349. In his timely book on *Existenzerfahrung und Religion* (Mainz, 1968), K. Riesenhuber locates the foundations of the philosophy of religion in human existential experience. Compare also Karl Rahner's deliberations on man's existential experience of transcendence, for example, in *Hearers of the Word* (London and Sydney, 1969), also the counterarguments of J. B. Metz, for example in *Theology of the World* (New York, 1969).

8   H. Nakamura stresses the existential character of the Buddhist experience in his summary "Grundlehren des Buddhismus," *Buddhismus der Gegenwart,* pp. 15f., 20ff., 26ff., 31, 33f.

9   The teaching on impermanence derives from the first of the "Four Noble Truths." The sense of the ephemeral character of life pervades the entire Japanese medieval literature inspired by Buddhism.

10   A Chinese Zen master asks, "And what about one who has died the great death only to gain life?" W. Gundert clarifies this. "Even one who reads the question superficially will understand that the sole point here is the 'great death' that everyone willing to gain true life and freedom must once undergo. To be sure, the critic can retort that in that case nobody really dies. Nevertheless, there exist people, not only those rooted in Buddhism, who suddenly one day lose all they have and all they are and experience the loss as a death . . . And as much as one is prone to erect 'necessary' and unsurmountable walls between Christianity and Buddhism, we in turn can ask, who, in regard to his human experience and behavior toward this authentic Christianity, has the wider path at his disposal—the one who has died the great death, in the sense of the Zen master Dschau-dschou, or the Christian for whom such words are empty meanings." From *Bi-yän-lu: Niederschrift von der smaragdenen Felswand,* vol. II (Munich, 1967), pp. 159, 169f.

11   Cf. Teilhard de Chardin's first memorandum to Auguste Valensin, dated 12 December 1919, in *Maurice Blondel-Pierre Teilhard de Chardin: Briefwechsel,* edited with commentary by Henri de Lubac (Freiburg and Munich, 1967), p. 30. In the commentary, de Lubac refers to our passage from "La Messe sur le Monde" (1923); see p. 75.

12   According to Buddhist tradition, the Buddha's last words to his disciples were "Strive with earnestness." The point of this exhortation is, of course, the earnestness of striving for salvation. The teachings of the Buddha do not constitute an ethic or a philosophy, but rather a path to salvation. Can we not say the same of Christianity?

13   Traditional sayings of Zen masters such as "Think not of good, think not of evil," are intended to exclude all dualistic thinking, not to deny morality in an antinomian fashion. Observance

of the Buddhist commandments is always presupposed. "The easy way to become a Buddha" begins with the effort "not to do evil" —so Dōgen's *Shōbōgenzō, The Book of Life and Death.*

14   A popular Buddhist saying is:

> *"Hard is to be born into human life,*
> *We now live it.*
> *Difficult is it to hear the teaching of the Buddha,*
> *We now hear it.*
> *If we do not deliver ourselves in this present life,*
> *No hope is there ever to cross the sea of birth and*
>   *death.*
> *Let us all together, with the truest heart,*
> *Take refuge in the Three Treasures!"*

15   Quoted from *Buddhist Texts through the Ages,* ed. Edward Conze (Oxford, 1954 and New York, 1964), pp. 52, 54.

16   Cf. Māhaprajñāpāramitopadeśa, Book 1, quoted in Masao Abe, "Gendai ni okeru 'shin' no mondai" ("The Question of Faith in Modern Times"), The Japanese Buddhist Society, ed. *Bukkyō ni okeru 'shin' no mondai* (Tokyo, 1963 and 1970), p. 21.

17   *Ibid.,* Book 6.

18   Majjhima-nikāya I, 36-38, in Conze, *op. cit.,* pp. 52, 53.

19   Cf. Abhidharmakosha Book 4, and on the commentary see S. Matsunami, "Bukkyō ni okeru shin no chii" ("The Place of Faith in Buddhism"), *op. cit.,* p. 48.

20   *Ibid.* Matsunami investigates the teaching on faith in the 6th book of Jōyuishikiron.

21   *Ibid.,* p. 49f. The Mahāyānasraddhotpadaśāstra, Book 4, as its title suggests, treats practice and faith.

22   Compare Heinrich Dumoulin, "Buddha-Symbole und Buddha-Kult," *Religion und Religionen: Festschrift Gustav Mensching* (Bonn, 1967), pp. 50-63.

23   Tannishō, Book 6. See also the penetrating study of faith and grace in Shinran by A. Bloom, *Shinran's Gospel of Pure Grace* (Tucson, 1965).

24   Majjhima-nikāya I, 479-480, in Conze, *Buddhist Texts through the Ages,* p. 52.

25   Niwano Nikkyō, the president of the Buddhist new religion, *Risshō Kōseikai,* devoted himself to copying the three Lotus Sutras for 83 days, before placing the great Buddha statue in the new buildings of his cult.

26   Matsunami, *op. cit.,* p. 56.

27   In his well known work *Buddhism* (Oxford, 1951), Conze puts the question, "Is Buddhism atheistic?" He goes on to distinguish three meanings of the term and argues that while there is no personal Creator-God in Buddhism, it is possible to conceive of an impersonal or supra-personal Godhead:

> When we compare the attributes of the Godhead as they are understood by the more mystical tradition of Christian thought, with those of Nirvāna, we find almost no difference at all . . . we are told that Nirvāna is permanent, stable, imperishable, immovable, ageless, deathless, unborn, and unbecome, that it is power, bliss and happiness, the secret refuge, the shelter, and the place of unassailable safety; that it is the real Truth and supreme Reality, that it is the Good, the supreme goal and the one and only consummation of our life, the eternal, hidden and incomprehensible Peace. [p. 38ff.]

Christmas Humphreys, in this regard, writes that "as between the theist and atheist positions, Buddhism is atheist," but a few lines later he qualifies this by saying that "The Buddhist teaching on God, in the sense of ultimate Reality, is neither agnostic, as is sometimes claimed, nor vague, but clear and logical. Whatever Reality may be, it is beyond the conception of the finite intellect . . ." From *Buddhism* (London, 1951), p. 79. Winston King, in his *Buddhism and Christianity, Some Bridges of Understanding* (London, 1963), p. 37, also takes up the problem and speaks of a "divine," or "spiritual" or "religious atheism" in contradistinction to any purely materialistic conception of the universe. He goes on (pp. 38ff.) to examine four factors which in his view form a "reality-complex" or "reality-structure," "namely, Dharma, Karma,

Nirvāna and the Buddha," and which might fulfill a God-function in Buddhism. Regarding the Buddha, he says "Buddha-veneration often approaches theistic adoration in quality" (p. 85).

28   In his essay on the main teachings of Buddhism, Hajime Nakamura distinguishes between the "empirical self in daily life" and the "religious self." In his view we may "conclude that the realization of Nirvāna can be explained in other words as taking refuge in self." Nakamura, *op. cit.,* p. 20.

29   The concept of experience is broad and multifaceted. Above (note 8), we treated existential experience. The particular experience of transcendence includes, on the subjective side, a cognitive and a receptive moment, and points to transcendent reality.

30   Udāna 80-81; Conze, *Buddhist Texts through The Ages,* p. 95.

31   Nakamura, *op. cit.,* p. 27.

32   Winston King touches upon the problem of the particular religious category of the Buddha and writes: "This is a universe, in which occurs the 'incarnation' of Buddhas for men and their salvation." He goes on to ask, "Is there an overarching Mercy that brings forth or incarnates itself in Buddhahood periodically? Is there some ineluctable necessity in the nature of things that produces such individuals in 'the fulness of time'?" *op. cit.,* p. 55. This question takes various turns respectively in Southern or Theravāda Buddhism and in Northern or Mahāyāna Buddhism, and is not easy to answer in a simple or generally satisfactory manner. A passage in the Pāli canon describes the indescribable essence of the Buddha as follows:

> A Tathagata is a seer of what is to be seen, but he does not mind the seen, the unseen, the seeable, the seer. So likewise with the heard, the sensed and the cognized: he thinks of none of these modes of theirs. Therefore among things seen, heard, sensed and cognized he is precisely 'such' (*tadi*). Moreover, than he who is 'such' there is no other 'such' further or more excellent.

From Conze, *Buddhist Texts through the Ages,* p. 108: Anguttaranikāya II, 25.

33   Chapter 16. The expression in the sutra (Chinese-Japanese: *kuon jitsujō*), according to the Buddhist encyclopedia, signifies that "Shākyamuni, who in Bodhgaya, India, became enlightened under the tree of enlightenment, is only a temporary appearance. In reality he attained enlightenment in the eternal past and became Buddha; ever since then, in the great expanse of time, he has taught mankind." See *Shin-Bukkyō Jiten,* ed. Hajime Nakamura (Tokyo, 1962), p. 127.

34   Compare for example the sculptures in the Lahore museum (Gandhāra style, 2nd to 4th centuries) and in the Calcutta museum (the schools of Sārnāth, 5th century); see the prints in *The Way of Buddha,* II (Ministry of Information and Broadcasting, Government of India, 1956), No. 29 and 30. Compare also the description of the miracle in A. de Silva-Vigier, *The Life of Buddha* (London, 1955), p. 40.

35   For example, Kōshō Otani, the heir to the Eastern Honganji Temple of the Shin School in Kyoto. See his series of articles, "Shin to no taiwa" ("Conversation with Faith"), *Daihōrin* (1970), esp. the June issue, pp. 58, 60.

36   Cf. "Technique and Personal Devotion in the Zen Exercise," *Studies in Japanese Culture,* ed. J. Roggendorf (Tokyo 1963), pp. 17-40.

CHAPTER 4

Buddhist
Spirituality and Mysticism

Spirituality is profoundly significant for the interreligious dialogue. Each of the religions actually engaged in dialogue has a fundamental (if sometimes hidden) basis in spirituality. Moreover, it is this basis which offers the most intimate point of contact between the adherents of different religions. In our discussion of the dialogue with the Buddhists, we discovered that religious experience makes it possible to establish connections where doctrines stand in irreconcilable opposition to each other.

In the scholarly investigation of Buddhist teachings, the impression is easily created that there exists an unbridgeable gulf between Buddhism and Christianity, a

111

gap excluding any hope of genuine dialogue. And in fact, Western Buddhology long held that the two religions were diametrically opposed. The accentuated rationality of Buddhist teachings forced scholars to this conclusion, both for the pessimistically inclined forms of early Indian Buddhism still present in today's Theravāda and for the monistic speculations of Mahāyāna. In either case, a chasm separated Buddhism and Christianity.

Nevertheless, soon after the Second Vatican Council, the dialogue between the two got underway. And both sides recognized that it would be to their advantage, at least at the outset, to avoid discussion of doctrinal tenets and begin instead with the actual experiences of religious life. Because of this, spirituality and mysticism emerged as the central themes of the dialogue. Doctrinal systems play a minor role in Buddhism in any case, since Buddhism is based on experience. Moreover, seen in the light of spirituality, many teachings present new perspectives. Today the special significance of spirituality for the interreligious dialogue can be regarded as an accepted fact.

As a result, there has been a great deal of serious endeavor on the part of Christians to gain a deeper insight into the spirituality of Buddhism. It is not merely a question of obtaining useful information (though that, of course, is indispensable for conducting a dialogue), but also of discovering what can be learned from Buddhist spirituality. We are convinced that the Divine Spirit is at work in all religions and the good that can be found in all religions derives from the Spirit of God. In a number of undertakings (for example, in the efforts of Father Enomiya-Lassalle to make Zen meditation fruitful for Christian spirituality) learning is undoubtedly the predominant motive. This chapter, however, attempts to present a more general picture of the main tendencies and values of Buddhist spirituality, even though the enormous variety of phenomena within the greatly divergent forms of Buddhism makes a general description difficult. Naturally, these phenomena differ not only in meaning and content but also in value.

Almost all valuable tendencies in the spirituality of Buddhism are more or less closely related to the basic themes of original Buddhism. This original Buddhism, as many of today's Buddhists have discovered anew, represents the essence of Buddhism in its purest form.[1] We will be in close touch with the Buddhist movement of our times if we examine some of the fundamental traits of Buddhist spirituality which were prominent in early Buddhism and have remained influential ever since. These basic traits are related to the essential character of Buddhism as a religion of salvation, specifically, a religion of salvation from man's existential suffering. Because of this fundamental disposition, Buddhism gives rise to the practical spirituality founded on existential experience. I shall discuss first the existential spirituality of practical life peculiar to Buddhism. In a second part of the chapter, I shall examine the Buddhist mode of salvation through knowledge and the meditation which is an essential element of all forms of Buddhist spirituality. In particular I shall examine this meditation as it relates to conscious rationality, metaphysical thinking and intuitive enlightenment. In this context, finally, I shall touch on Buddhist mysticism.

The Existential Spirituality of Practical Life

A conspicuous trait in the character of the Buddha was his attitude of reserve, if not outright rejection, toward speculative thinking. Shākyamuni, if we can

trust the accounts in the Pāli canon, kept himself aloof
from the doctrinal disputations so much in vogue in the
India of his time and did not respond to metaphysical
questions. His concern was of a practical nature. Because he met men in a state of suffering, his desire was
to help them escape from their existential situation.
This cannot be achieved by any kind of cogitation but
is a practical matter, just as is the physician's help for
the sick—a favorite comparison of Shākyamuni. The
Buddha has illustrated the urgency of this help in many
parables stressing the moral that all depends on the
individual's own effort.[2] He introduced his disciples to
a practical spirituality. They were to spare no effort in
order to obtain deliverance from this existential state
of suffering, irrespective of whether they conceived this
goal as the extinction of the painful terrestrial existence
or as the attainment of the "other shore" of peace and
happiness.

"Useful for oneself—Useful for others"

The practical trait observable in Shākyamuni characterizes all forms of Buddhist spirituality. In Indian Buddhism, with its emphasis on the dark and painful, the
spiritual exertion is directed toward the eradication of
suffering and its causes. In the other forms of Buddhism, the gloomy shadows are not completely dis-
pelled, but deliverance takes on more of the meaning
of a positive fulfillment. Whereas original Buddhism
experienced salvation as liberation from the existential
situation of suffering, in subsequent interpretations it is
given a wider significance and encompasses everything
useful for man.

Later Buddhist scholasticism summarizes its teaching on usefulness in the all-embracing formula *ātma-hitam para-hitam* (Japanese: *jiri rita*), literally "Useful for oneself—useful for others." The Bodhisattva ideal was an exemplification of this formula in as much as the Bodhisattva, who has attained enlightenment, possesses the maximum of "usefulness for oneself" and at the same time helps all other living beings. The first part of the formula—"useful for oneself"—signified for Mahāyāna Buddhists the spirituality of the "Minor Vehicle" (*Hīnā-yana*) while its second part—"useful for others"—denotes the Mahāyāna ideal, the salvation of all living beings.[3] The Zen Buddhists in particular emphasize the close connection between the two parts and seek their ultimate identity in accord with the Bodhisattva ideal.[4] The Bodhisattva, who has attained the full measure of his own perfection, never ceases to be of service to all living beings. It should be noted that usefulness at the core of the formula demonstrates the practical, pragmatic character of Buddhist spirituality derived from existential experience.

The goal of the self-focused spirituality of ancient Buddhism is the ideal of the "saint" (Sanskrit: *Arhat*) who, by his own merits, has reached a state of perfection worthy of veneration and free from all desire and from the cycle of reincarnations. The spiritual exercises leading to this perfection are minutely described in the Pāli canon; they form the well-known meditative-ascetic spirituality still practiced today in the Theravāda monasteries. The meritorious observation of the rules ensures the practical usefulness of this kind of spirituality, but because this usefulness has little to do with the world outside the monasteries, Theravāda spirituality remains largely confined to the monks. Only a relatively small number of laymen try to adapt themselves to the

rigorous monastic discipline. The large majority of laymen practice Buddhism in the form of a popular religion. They find the fulfillment of their religious needs
in the supplement to Buddhism provided by the autoch-
thonous cults which have been absorbed into the popular Buddhism of all Theravāda countries. These elements stemming from popular religiosity are obviously
of practical usefulness for the individual as well as the
community, and they serve to alleviate the sufferings
and evils of human existence.

"Useful for others," the second point of the directive
formula, is understood by Mahāyāna Buddhism to
mean useful for universal salvation. Naturally, one's
own self is included in the intended state of universal
perfection, the attainment of Buddhahood. Numerous
religious exercises and devotional practices, representing many stages of religious reflection, are aimed at this
goal. Prostrating oneself and burning incense before the
image of Buddha, venerating the Bodhisattvas, reciting
the sutras and invoking the name of Buddha, pronounc-
ing the Bodhisattva vows and performing penitential
rituals and magic rites, chanting *mantra* formulas—all
of these exercises are intended as practical actions for
bringing about some good and useful result. The result
may be of a material nature (such as healing a disease,
obtaining children or an abundant crop), but even if the
intended result is spiritual, it usually remains within the
confines of this world. This is true to a certain extent
even of the meditative exercises. The psychic equilibrium and the inner harmony obtained in meditation can
be of great help to man in his earthly existence, and
Buddhists praise the experiences of enlightenment on
account of their life-enriching and self-expanding effects.

The only important exception in this regard is the

Amida religion, which differs from other forms of Buddhism in several respects. Amida spirituality draws its basic inspiration from the vivid representations of the "Pure Land" ruled by the Buddha Amitābha. Many devotees of Amida maintain a personal relationship with their Buddha, in whom they seek help and salvation not only during their earthly life, but above all in the hour of their death, the moment of possible rebirth into the Pure Land. To be sure, Buddhists have only vague ideas about the Pure Land, and the moderns often think of it in mythical terms. It is not essentially different from the general Buddhist conception of the "other shore," a parabolic term rich in suggestion. Man can have no clear and precise knowledge of the other shore.

Many more illustrations could be provided from Mahāyāna (which, like Theravāda, contains accretions from indigenous religions) in order to demonstrate the pragmatic nature of Buddhist spirituality. Suffice it to draw attention to the Japanese new religions of Buddhist lineage which represent contemporary examples of this tendency in Buddhism. All these new religions recommend a practical spirituality. Western commentators have censured the best-known and most influential of these popular religions, the Sōka-Gakkai movement, for distorting the classical triad of the True, the Good, and the Beautiful, into the formula of the Beautiful, the Useful and the Good in order to fit their own pragmatic value-creating theory. It cannot be denied that at the time of its rapid expansion, the Sōka-Gakkai movement overstepped the limits of the permissible in praising the "Divine favors" (*go riyaku*). But it should not be forgotten that the emphasis on the practical and life-enriching usefulness of religious practices agrees with the most orthodox Buddhist tradition. The works

on human life (Japanese: *jinseiron*), authored by the
Sōka-Gakkai's third president, Daisaku Ikeda, avoid
the extremes and offer a Buddhist view on life saturated
with religious sentiments.[5]

Morality, Commandments and Compassion

As the history of religions has shown, no religion
completely lacks the ethical dimension of practical
spirituality. Buddhist ethics has commanded less attention by Western scholars than Buddhist spirituality for
two reasons. First, to a large extent it coincides with
the so-called natural laws of general human morality.
Second, within the Buddhist body of doctrines it claims
no independent place. All forms of Buddhism recognize
the Buddhist Five Precepts as the foundation of moral
life. Usually these are formulated in the negative as
prohibitions—not to kill, not to steal, not to commit
sexual misconduct, not to lie, and not to take any intox-
icating liquor or drugs. In ancient Buddhism, in addition to these precepts, a large number of proscriptions
or regulations were observed in monastic life; but those
rules, though even today observed in Theravāda monasteries, are not considered morally binding by the large
majority of Buddhists. Still characteristic of Buddhism
is the teaching of the "three poisons" (Japanese: *sandoku*) based on early scriptures. These three—greed,
hate, and ignorance (stupidity or delusion)—poison the
good roots in man.[6] Thus, in addition to the evil passions of greed and hate, the formula names ignorance,
a dynamic link in the twelve-part chain of causation
which is relevant more existentially than ethically.

The culmination of Buddhist morality in compassion

transcends the ethical realm. Compassion is not merely an ethical virtue; it includes an attitude which the Buddhist has a task of developing during his lifetime. It is the goal of his moral effort, and at the same time the precondition for and the fruit of meditation, and is essentially connected with the path of salvation.

Compassion is the Buddhist attitude most comparable to the Christian commandment of love for one's neighbor. Yet, on comparison of the two, considerable differences appear. Philosophically, the Christian love of neighbor is understood in terms of the Occidental concept of the person. Theologically it derives from the love of God, which together with it constitutes the whole commandment of Christian love. In Buddhism not only is there no vertical relation to a personal Supreme Being, but in addition interhuman behavior is not conceived of as a relation between persons. Moreover, in Buddhism, the personal dignity of humans is further obscured by including animals as sentient beings equally deserving of compassion.

Ancient Indian Buddhism primarily connected compassion and meditation with the four Brahma stages or abodes (*brahma-vihāra.*) In the first three stages compassionate behavior is set forth as kindness (Pāli: *mettā*), compassion in the strict sense, (Pāli: *karunā*) evoked by the human condition of suffering (*dukkha*), and shared joy (Pāli: *muditā*). These three are subsumed under the fourth and highest stage, equanimity (Pāli: *upekkhā*), and thus the behavior of love for neighbor is subordinated within the procedure of meditation.[7]

In Mahāyāna Buddhism, compassion is the characteristic virtue of the Bodhisattva who postpones his own entrance into Nirvāna in order to lead all sentient beings to salvation. Compassion is thus linked to the altruistic ideal of being "useful for others." The Bodhisattva embodies that behavior of mutual kindness and loving compassion which, according to the Mahāyānistic understanding, incorporates every moral perfection worth striving for. This behavior is signified in Japanese by the word *ji-hi,* consisting of two Chinese ideograms and combining the two Pāli concepts of *mettā* (Sanskrit: *maitrī*[8] or *maitreya*) and *karunā.* Among Far Eastern Mahāyāna Buddhists, the word *jihi* has a very comprehensive meaning and wide application. Many Japanese Buddhists regard *jihi* as the quintessence of their religious life.

Here we clearly encounter one important point about the often observed discrepancy between Buddhism as it is lived and Buddhism as it is explained philosophically. For Buddhist philosophical analysis would dissolve the object of compassion, the concrete other, into its components or prove it essentially empty in the sense of the *sūnya* doctrine. But the Buddhist saturated with his religion concretely practices compassion every day a number of times. Here life as it is lived is to be preferred over metaphysical speculation, even though the latter also contributes to the theme of compassion.[9]

Buddhist spirituality emphasizes compassion a great deal. The author of a Japanese introduction to Buddhism directed to a wide audience, including intellectuals, writes that "In Mahāyāna Buddhism, compassion (*jihi*) is the foundation of all . . . but the teaching on compassion did not wait until the appearance of Mahāyāna; rather it is fully presented in the words and deeds of Shākyamuni. Over and above any difference between Mahāyāna and Hīnayāna, all who follow the teachings of the Buddha must without exception realize the virtue of compassion."[10] Then in a series of quotations from the Buddhist canon, the author shows how the practice of *jihi* begins with overcoming hate and animosity, is expressed in an unconditional respect for life in all of its forms, excludes violence, and furthers gentleness, kindness and sincere generosity. He interprets Shākya-muni's exhortation to continual effort, directed to his disciples at the hour of entering Nirvāna, as an impera-tive command to practice compassion.

Compassion proves to be a total, existential manner of behavior strived for by the Buddhist but not easily explicable in philosophic terms. The moral relevance of this manner of behavior is obvious enough. If it is close to the Christian love of neighbor, the primary reason is that the Buddhist usually, if not always, makes his all-important decision of conscience in concrete relation to his fellow man. Buddhist compassion is ultimately part of the path of salvation and must be understood from that perspective.

Consciousness of Sin and Repentance

Just as ethics claims no independent place in the Buddhist path of salvation, so too the essentially moral qualities of the sense of sin, guilt, repentance and for-giveness are not of primary importance in Buddhism according to Buddhist doctrine. To find counterparts to the Christian sense of sin, however, we would do well to recall the Buddhist view of human existence. One can rightly see a similarity between that "suffering" (Pāli: *dukkha*) which in original Buddhism is tantamount to human existence, and the sinful human condition which for Christians results from "original sin" and personal fault. More evident yet is the analogy to sin in the Buddhist concepts of ignorance (Pāli: *avijjā*) and thirst or desire (Pāli: *tanhā*), and in the comprehensive karma-structure, when these are seen as the roots of all suffering. Thus the Buddhist conception, similar to the Christian teachings on sin, accounts for important elements of human experience. But, strictly speaking, the Buddhist account appears to leave little room for personal responsibility and freedom. At this point, the interreligious dialogue can all too easily come to a standstill, even though Buddhism in practice has never denied freedom and responsibility in moral action.

Turning to the practice of Buddhism, one can observe that various forms of sin-consciousness and repentance have from early times widely influenced the whole of Buddhism. Not all expressions of the repentance of sin are of equal importance; some remain external and conventional formulas, and others diminish the moral significance through philosophies alien to the notion of person. Since we are here dealing with psychic processes as well, the clarification of this complex matter is all the more difficult. Nevertheless, a brief look at Buddhist exercises of repentance can both inform us of significant factors and open new doors to dialogue.

The observance of confession by early Buddhist monks, as reported in the Pāli canon, must be understood in terms of Buddhist monasticism.[11] The ceremony took place twice a month, in the evening on the days of full moon and new moon. Its motive was the assurance of complete and unconditional observance of monastic discipline. The monks assiduously observed a large number of proscriptions, and when any monk transgressed against any one of them, he would accuse himself before the assembly of his confreres. Most of the proscriptions concerned matters of living in the cloistered community, but they included the main Buddhist commandments as well and their transgression also was a matter for confession. Further, it may be noted that the monks, "having left their houses and chosen to live without a home" (a formula of ancient Buddhist scriptures), voluntarily took upon themselves the burden of the rules of the order and no doubt felt an inner obligation to observe them. The moral importance attributed to the observance of a rule would always depend, of course, on the spiritual state of the particular monastery. Accordingly, the degrees of consciousness of sin and repentance would vary. Confession of sin forms the core of the Buddhist practice of penitence, but it cannot be fully performed without an avowal of guilt. Canonical scriptures stress that the effect of this practice is purification. The confessional ceremony is even today an integral part of monastic spirituality in Theravāda Buddhism.

In contrast to the early Indian version of penitence, where the emphasis was on the confession of sin, Far Eastern Mahāyāna Buddhism has stressed the need for repentance. Buddhist repentance, along with the exercises and rites coupled with it, is signified by the Chinese-Japanese word *sange*. This word consists of two ideograms, the second of which literally means "repentance" and, in Buddhist context, "amelioration for the future" as well. Ancient texts speak of "shame" and "remorse"; those who "wear the dress of shame" because of evil deeds of their past, feel shame toward themselves, toward others, toward heaven and men.

In Mahāyāna Buddhism there has evolved a great number of rites of repentance, varying according to the school and the preferred sutras, but in the main quite similar to one another. None includes a detailed confession of transgressions committed.[12] The repentance expressed refers primarily to the general sinful condition of man. In the course of religious decline during the Middle Ages in Japan, the rites of repentance were secularized. No longer did they serve to cleanse one of his sins; rather they were performed to gain earthly favors. At the same time, an increasing number of magical rites were incorporated.

The rituals of repentance were understood in terms of the monistic metaphysics of Mahāyāna Buddhism. The predominant *Tendai* teaching of the Middle Ages in Japan distinguished between a phenomenal and an absolute repentance, in alignment with the phenomenal and the absolute aspects of reality. In Zen Buddhism, this distinction is met under the terms of actual versus essential repentance.[13] Essential or absolute repentance grasps the oneness of reality. Identical with the knowledge brought by enlightenment, it sees through the original emptiness of all things in this world of appearance, including the emptiness of evil deeds committed. This mode of "repentance" cannot properly be called repentance in the strict sense of the word, since it does not immediately reflect the moral aspect of human existence. In contradistinction to "absolute repentance," that which Zen calls "actual repentance" pertains to all evil deeds arising from bad karma or producing bad karma. Such sins are easily detected by man as a daily occurrence in this world. The exercises and rites of repentance involve these sins, which are accounted for in the context of the teaching on karma. According to its inexorable law, good deeds bear good fruit and evil deeds bear bad fruit; but in practice the karmic law does not necessarily exclude personal responsibility. The Buddhist, reciting the formula for the ritual of repentance, promises "not to commit evil deeds again." Thus he literally expresses his resolution to act morally. The Zen master's frequent admonitions to repent, like the traditional sermons on penitence by Buddhist monks of all schools, imply that those addressed are free to decide

their way. Not until modern times did Buddhists encounter the problem of determinism, and they have
generally answered in favor of human freedom.[14]

In Amida Buddhism, consciousness of sin is especially prevalent, though the account of sin and repentance hardly differs from that of other Buddhist schools.
As in all forms of Buddhism, the fact of human sin is
explained in terms of involvement in bad karma; occasionally, the sinfulness of human nature and the com-
mission of conscious sinful deeds are also spoken of.[15]
Shinran, the founder of the Japanese Pure Land School,
appears to have considerably underestimated freedom
of will, if not denied it outright, as a result of his distrust
of human self-determination. His extreme awareness of
sin made him believe that he was not capable of any
good deed. Masaharu Anesaki has noted that "his
teachings left room for an indulgent tendency to creep
into religion."[16] Still, Amidism in Japan did not degenerate into total amoralism.

Our considerations have led us to an account of some,
though certainly not all, of the various manifestations
of sin and repentance in rites and individual practice.
Their enormous variety and widespread occurrence in
all forms of Buddhism force us to recognize that Buddhism has by no means omitted the phenomenon of
human sin, that in practice sin is deeply felt and constantly combated. And if the Buddhist answer to the
problem of sin appears complex and somewhat obscure,
one need only recall the Pauline doctrine of the "mystery of evil" (2 Thess. II, 7) and the inadequacy of any
smooth and rationalistic solution.

The consciousness of sin and the phenomenon of repentance in Buddhism fit into the total structure of
concrete religious experience. This structure is the comprehensive experience of the suffering and imperma-

nence of human existence. It is exemplified by the early Buddhist notion of *dukkha,* which apparently contains the particular experience of sin as understood in the West.[17] If it is difficult to point out personal elements in the Buddhist consciousness of sin and practice of repentance, this is undoubtedly because of the obscurity of the personal dimension in that religion. In the next chapter I shall examine this problem in more detail.

In spite of this obscurity, one can occasionally note personal attitudes in Buddhist prayers of repentance. It is true that the Buddhist seldom prays verbally, but formulated prayers do occur in various forms of Buddhism.[18] We may perceive, for example, a covert note of remorse and a plea for forgiveness along with the obvious indigence of the figure praying at the symbolic footprints of the Buddha, or prostrate before a stupa, so often represented in the sculptures of early Buddhist Indian art.[19]

Generally speaking, the intensity of Buddhist penitential exercises both in rites of the cult and in individual practice permit us to conclude that personal commitment is in fact present. One can still witness intensive exercises of devotion, truly inspired by a penitential spirit, in present day Buddhist monasteries in Asia. To be sure, Buddhists do not anticipate renewal merely from the exercise of repentance. For meditation and introspection are held to be equally, if not more effective. Moreover, the Buddhist recognizes a practical guidance which, while embedded in religion, leaves room for common sense. A newspaper of the Amida school once printed an answer to a mother worried about her errant daughter and seeking advice. The answer tells the mother not to fret about the past, but rather—now that she has been made aware of "the perversion of her blind love"—to consider wherein true love resides. "He who is awakened . . . to the great mercy of the Buddha does not idly dwell on sins and mistakes of the past. Rather, the more he recognizes the degree of his sinful involvement in karma, the more thankful he is to receive the great mercy of the Buddha." As a response to the wayward behavior of her daughter, the mother is advised to express compassion and to send the daughter to friends or relatives in a place where she can more easily find her way back to a good life.[20]

In order to assess this complex consciousness of sin and the exercise of repentance in Buddhism, it is essential that we consider all of the various factors in relation to their religious value. Christians can learn much from the practical Buddhist attitude, especially once they have understood that an excessive consciousness of sin in the West has frequently led to unbearable difficulties now treated by psychotherapists. Many painful conflicts would be avoided or resolved if only the persons concerned could experience the profound, inner stillness of meditation and gain new self-confidence. The pastoral advice of the Amida Buddhist to the heartbroken mother contains a bit of wisdom one would do well to consider. A problem so deeply rooted in man's existence, so complex as sin, repentance and inner renewal, cannot be approached merely theoretically, but demands that we give full attention to practical experience as well.

The existential orientation of the practice of Buddhist spirituality offers many points of contact for the interreligious dialogue. Two deserve particular attention. First, the priority given to practical spiritual experience over theory is an important fact. Buddhists want to find in the Christian partner of the dialogue a religious man who, although practicing a different form of devotion, possesses a sympathetic understanding of Buddhist piety. Second, the significance of the pragmatic element for the dialogue must be recognized. In the encounter of the different spiritualities, the results which allow a conclusion about the value of spiritual attitudes obviously are the first thing to attract attention. Wherever the results reveal something valuable, circumspection is appropriate, for here a door opens to penetration into unknown regions.

Salvation Based on Knowledge

In the first part of our considerations, we discussed the broad stream of practical Buddhist piety which undertakes to save man lost in the cycle of rebirth and to heal, enrich and give happiness to suffering and despairing human beings. By putting the accent on the practical usefulness of religious practices, we were also able to acknowledge the role of popular piety in Buddhism. The latter has often been disregarded in the discussions of Buddhist spirituality, even though religious life in the Buddhist countries of Asia is largely shaped by popular beliefs and customs. We ought at least to mention that popular piety also reaches into higher regions and that, contrariwise, the higher spirituality which we might call mysticism in the wider sense extends into popular piety. We could have ventured an excursion into mysticism in the first part of our considerations, had we dealt with shamanism, which even today is of some significance in the popular piety of Buddhism. But here we must be content with stating it as a fact.

In the second part of our considerations, we can again choose as our point of departure the basic nature of the religion of salvation discernible in original Buddhism. In ancient India, the religious ways of salvation were divided into "ways of loving surrender" (*bhakti-mārga*), "ways of ritual observance" or "of action" (*karma-mārga*), and "ways of cognition" (*jnāna-mārga*). In this classification, the Buddhist path of salvation would belong to the "ways of cognition." Ignorance (Sanskrit: *avidyā*, Japanese: *mumyō*), the first link in the Buddhist "chain of causation" (Sanskrit: *pratītya-samutpāda;* Japanese: *juni inen*), also known as the formula of "conditioned co-production" or "conditioned genesis," sets into motion the cycle of rebirth full of suffering. Correspondingly, ultimate and definitive deliverance is achieved through liberating knowledge. For the Buddhist, the peerless supreme enlightenment experienced by the Buddha under the Bodhi tree is an example of the highest possible religious knowledge. In Buddhism, knowledge is associated with meditation, but knowledge as well as meditation has assumed various forms in the different Buddhist schools.

Rationality and Buddhist Gnosis

There were two main Buddhist branches which in the past were generally called the "Minor Vehicle" (*Hīnayāna*) and the "Major Vehicle" (*Mahāyāna*). The first of these, ancient Indian Buddhism (including several ancient Buddhist schools which are now extinct in addition to the Theravāda of Ceylon and Southeast Asia, conceived saving knowledge chiefly as a kind of cognition in which man perceives not only his existential situation in suffering, but also the universe and all things (*dharmas*) in the universe. Saving knowledge contains the perception of one's own earlier existences as well as of the cycle of reincarnations of the innumerable beings living in the "six ways."[21] Its foremost object, however, is the Four Holy Truths, i.e., the truths of suffering, of the origination of suffering, of the cessation of suffering, and the way that leads to the cessation of suffering. This knowledge is described as a conscious, clear, and rational cognition which dissects reality into its components; this process of rational thinking is at the service of the liberating knowledge.

Rationality is an obvious trait of the way of knowledge described in the Pāli canon; indeed, rationality is characteristic of all Buddhism and is an integral part of the Buddhist's spiritual attitude. It is true that the rational element receded with the increasing distance of Buddhism from its Indian origins, yet it never entirely disappeared. Chinese and Japanese Buddhism also have their share of contributions to philosophic thought, recorded in the cultural history of these peoples. One may say without exaggeration that wherever Buddhism spread, great significance in religious effort was given to knowledge.

Particularly noteworthy in this respect is the process of modernization in contemporary Buddhism. Here, as in all such attempts at modernization in the great religions of today, rationality is a principal driving force. Contemporary Buddhist scholars emphasize the important role which the original teaching of the chain of causation plays in the proper rational understanding of the Buddhist doctrine. This forms the basis of the various levels of speculation on Emptiness (Sanskrit: *sūnyatā,* Japanese: *kū*). As interpreted by Japanese Buddhist scholars, this formula not only relativizes all expressions and appearances in this phenomenal world, but also demonstrates the agreement of critical-rational

Buddhist teaching with modern natural science. A Japanese Buddhist drew an analogy between Emptiness (*sūnyatā*) and Planck's constant h, to demonstrate the rationality of his religious world-view.[22] Similar attempts have been made by the Buddhist scholars in the Theravāda countries who have tried to prove the harmony of the analytical and pluralistic Theravāda philosophy with the world-view of modern natural science. All these attempts in contemporary Buddhism have been inspired by the conviction of the basic rationality of the Buddhist way of salvation based on knowledge.

The secularized rationality of modern Buddhism obviously differs in essence from the liberating knowledge or the *Jnānic* efforts at salvation in early Buddhism described in the Pāli canon. Nevertheless, it probably proceeds from the same psychic roots; note the predilection for modern psychology and modern psychotherapeutic methods evinced by today's Buddhism in the process of secularization. In the light of the history of religion, the Buddhist way of liberating knowledge may reveal gnostic tendencies. Even the term "Buddhist *gnosis*" has been used. It seems inappropriate to place the Buddhist way of salvation side by side with the gnostic systems of salvation which emerged in the Hellenistic world, in dependence on and opposition to the revealed Judaeo-Christian religion. Buddhism should not even be considered as gnosticism in a wider sense. Nevertheless, in their origins, certain Buddhistic attitudes and inclinations show an affinity to gnosticism.

First of all, the basic theme of liberating knowledge is common to both. According to gnostic tenets, knowledge *as such* possesses the power of salvation. This knowledge is not received from outside, but constitutes an inseparable and hidden possession of man. Basically, the pearl and the treasure are one's own self whose original state is radiant knowledge. This state is regained by *gnosis,* knowledge which is identical with self-knowledge and includes knowledge of the world and knowledge of salvation. According to a leading authority, in *gnosis* "to know oneself" actually means "to recognize oneself, to rediscover and regain one's true 'self' which had been obscured by ignorance."[23] Undoubtedly, considerations such as self-salvation by self-knowledge developed in gnostic systems, can also be found in Buddhist schools. In the same way, Buddhism includes various forms of *esoterica;* for example, the distinction of a double truth, one for ordinary human beings and one for the enlightened; the communication of hidden knowledge reserved to the few, and so on. Hence, we are justified in speaking of gnostic tendencies in Buddhist spirituality. In his penetrating study on *gnosis,* J. A. Cuttat comes to the conclusion that its "affinity with the mental attitude of the ascetics of the Far East is evident."[24] A more detailed inquiry would reveal gnostic tendencies in most Buddhist branches of the Hīnayāna and the Mahāyāna as well as in the Tantric schools.

I would like to add two remarks which have a certain bearing on the interreligious dialogue. First, the gnostic attitude is basically different from the Christian attitude. For this reason, Cuttat has warned against the "gnostic temptation."[25] Today, this warning is all the more opportune since Christian circles, too, have shown a deplorable weakness for esoteric tendencies of a gnostic type. Furthermore—and I do not have time fully to explain this—the specifically gnostic attitudes, the attitude of self-redemption, the exclusive and one-sided esteem of knowledge, the tendency toward secrecy, and so on, can be impugned from a purely human and humanist as well as a Christian point of view.

Meditation and Mysticism

If all the gnostic movements in the history of religions contain hidden mystical elements, so we are able to discover expressions of Buddhist mysticism in what we called "Buddhist *gnosis.*" The evidences of this mysticism become clearer when we consider the Buddhist way of meditation. Meditation is at home in all branches of Buddhism; indeed, it is the heart of the religion of Buddha. The manner of meditation, of course, differs in method and value, but to recognize the existence of various methods is not to judge the quality of the experience achieved through a particular method. One person may achieve a deeper and more valuable experience through a generally less practiced method than another who makes use of one more used and more developed.

Ancient Buddhism took over such important elements as body-posture, breathing, and control of the senses, impressions and thoughts, from Yoga and integrated these into its manner of meditation.[26] Essentially exercises of concentration, emphasizing attention of the mind or mindfulness (Pāli: *sati*), these elements still flourish in Theravāda Buddhism. An important sutra text from the Pāli canon teaches attention to the body, the feelings, the states of consciousness and the objects of thought.[27] High levels of concentration are reached through this conscious mindfulness. Contrary to Zen meditation, this form is not non-representational, that is, without an object. Rather, it makes use of visual objects (Pāli: *kasina*) in fixing one's sight, and of images in concentrating with one's mental functions. The images may also inspire one to ponder, for example, the impermanence of earthly things, the frailty of human existence, and so on. Still, Buddhist meditation in general, in contrast to Christian meditation, reduces the importance of content in favor of the effort at concentration.[28]

Theravāda Buddhists consider their manner of meditation, with its roots in the ancient Pāli canon, the sole true and orthodox way, diametrically opposed to Christian prayer. Aware only of the anthropomorphic petition in Christianity, they reject this form of prayer as strongly as the thoroughly Christian notion (in their mind) of an anthropomorphic Creator-God. We shall return to this last point later.

Is the Buddhist way of meditation completely incompatible with Christian prayer? Certainly there are basic differences. Nevertheless, a common bond can be discovered. First of all, it can be said that Christian spirituality also strives for inner concentration, and that exercises of concentration neutral in content have their place in Christianity. Self-possession and self-control, achieved through concentration, are desirable assets for any religion; recognition of them can bring adherents of various religions to a common meeting-ground.

We can go a step further. Among the traditional forms of meditation in Theravāda spirituality, there is one exercise which one might say meets Christian prayer halfway. I refer to those meditative states in which the Buddhist monk extends his loving kindness and goodwill, his compassion, his sympathetic joy and his equanimity to all living beings, in the four directions of the universe, and is filled with the wish that all living beings live free from affliction and suffering, that all achieve the peace of Nirvāna.[29] This meditative wish is not directed to any higher being, but the one who performs it is certain that his wish will not be made in vain. What is the reason for his certainty? If it is rooted in trust that the meaning of the universe will ultimately be fulfilled, does this not point to an experience of transcendence? Is it not probable that the Buddhist monk in the force of these exercises touches upon something transcendent? Whatever the answer, I believe this kind of meditation approaches the Christian notion and practice of prayer. Certainly the Buddhist monk meditating in this way shows an attitude of great inner nobility.

The goal of the exercise of meditation in ancient Buddhism is Nirvāna—to be first attained not after death, but rather to the degree that experience can anticipate the state of Nirvāna in this present life. Both the state itself and the experience of Nirvāna in this life may be considered an experience of transcendence. Neither can be described adequately in words. The one who enjoys this experience is able to see through the impermanence of existing things and the insubstantiality of the self in intuitive clairvoyance (Pāli: *vipassanā*). He enjoys insight into the Four Holy Truths, which exhaust all truth. By the piercing insight into the Four Holy Truths, Nirvāna is attained. The experience is manifest through its effects—peace, joy, calm, and, at the height of the four levels of meditation (*jhāna*), the illimitable state of painless and joyless equanimity (*upekkhā*).

At the time of the increasing popularity of meditation in the West, encompassing all branches of Buddhism, Theravāda Buddhism has also adopted forms which deviate from those set down in the Pāli canon.[30] And all along the schools of Mahāyāna Buddhism have developed various methods of meditation. In the following we shall be concerned only with Zen meditation, not only because it is the most important form in the Mahāyāna Buddhism, but also because it most likely represents the apex of all Buddhist meditation.

Although the basic ideas of Mahāyāna were fully formulated in India, the particular school of Zen meditation emerged in China, where it was deeply influenced by the indigenous Taoism and from which it spread over all of East Asia—Korea, Japan, and Vietnam and Tibet as well. The Zen exercise of meditation may be described in terms of *zazen, kōan* and *satori. Zazen*, or sitting in the lotus posture, is done with short interruptions for an entire day during the *sesshin* or period of practice. In addition to these periods, eager disciples of Zen also sit an hour or more daily in *zazen.* Paradoxical questions or *kōan* put to the disciple help him concentrate until his mind is void of all thoughts, images and emotions, ideally to that extreme point where enlightenment or *satori* is suddenly and spontaneously experienced. The experience of enlightenment is ineffable; it penetrates to the depths of his being and transforms him.

In the past two or three decades there has appeared an immense number of publications on the way of Zen, incomparably more than in any other area in the study of Eastern religion. For this reason we can presuppose a general familiarity with this subject and proceed to highlight two points essential as much to the understanding of Buddhist spirituality and mysticism as to the interreligious dialogue. I refer first to the value of Zen meditation for the total psychosomatic integration of man, and second to the transcendental character of the experience of enlightenment. Today there is, for the most part, unanimous agreement on the first point. In distinction to the widespread mind-body duality in the

West, Eastern spirituality has dissolved the tension of mind and body in favor of a unity of the whole regulated by the spirit. And Zen has realized this resolution with inimitable mastery, both in its exercises and in life in general. For this reason, more and more Western people who have tried different forms of Eastern meditation are turning decisively to Zen. In Zen they have found the enrichment they sought for in their meditative life. In fact, many Christians, especially those belonging to contemplative religious orders, have adopted into their own spirituality Zen meditation with its sitting posture, breathing exercises and concentration aimed at Emptiness. Zen has been able to avoid the one-sided dangers of their forms of meditation.

The second point concerns the experience of enlightenment itself, and more precisely its relation to transcendence. Is the enlightenment attained through Zen meditation a genuine transcendental experience? In what way? In looking for an answer to these questions, the spiritual roots of the experience of Zen disciples must be taken into account. Their origin must be sought primarily in the teachings of the sutras of the "Perfection of Wisdom" (Sanskrit: *prajñā-pāramitā*) and the philosophy of Nāgārjuna. This doctrine has been interpreted in different ways by Buddhist and other scholars. Nāgārjuna has been called a rationalistic skeptic and even a nihilist, but he has also been counted among the great intuitive thinkers and philosophical mystics of mankind. The Japanese representatives of the Zen movement assert that Nāgārjuna upheld a new philosophical point of view rejecting both substantialism and nihilism.[31] By transcending being and nonbeing, he grasped the absolute reality transcending every duality. Although he never expressed his views on the supreme truth which he called Nothingness, it should not be given a nihilistic meaning. The Buddhists learnt from the silence of the Buddha; they do not offer pronouncements about the transcendental Absolute, but they do not deny it. In the preference for negation we can see a characteristic trait of Buddhist spirituality which reminds us of the *theologia negativa* of the Christian mystics. In addition to mystical intuition, Buddhism also makes use of a negative transcendental metaphysics. We shall return to this point in the last chapter.

No other contribution of Buddhism to the world's religious heritage has been as highly appreciated as Buddhist meditation. Friedrich Heiler, who in his time was only familiar with a part of the way of Buddhist meditation, still could contrast "Buddha, the master of concentration" and "Jesus, the master of prayer."[32] Meditation and prayer are not necessarily mutually exclusive; rather they can be seen as two related poles. These two preeminent forms of religious practice complement each other and together can bring about a higher state of perfection. In this manner, Eastern meditation can fulfill an important task in the West as well.

Today, as Buddhist meditation spreads throughout the world, it is at the same time being secularized. This process of secularization is not without its problems, particularly when Eastern or Buddhist meditation is coupled with psychedelic drugs. We cannot dismiss the questionable character of such practices as these, but not every form of secularization need be harmful. It is noteworthy that the secularization of Zen meditation began quite early, soon after Zen was introduced to Japan. Japanese Zen monasteries were quick to influence the cultural and artistic life of the land, and in this respect the monks incorporated worldly efforts into their religious concerns. By virtue of its humanistic qualities, Zen was able to plant seeds and reap harvests in many areas of Japanese culture. With this in mind, then, we cannot deprecate the fact that once again Zen is undergoing a secularization which engages it in the world.

Let us ask one last question, which will lead us back to the starting point of our investigations. How can meditation remain the heart and core of the Buddhist religion in spite of the secularization this meditation has undergone? Here we must once again consider the essence of Buddhist meditation. All forms of its practice essentially serve the objective of salvation. This is particularly evident when we consider the peak of experience attained through meditation, the insight or clairvoyance of Theravāda Buddhism and the enlightenment of Zen Buddhism. In each case, the experience is characterized by a cognitive element. In ancient Indian or Theravāda Buddhism, an intuitive knowledge of the Four Holy Truths accompanies the experience of Nirvāna. Mahāyāna Buddhism, including Zen, ascribes to enlightenment an activation of *prajñā*, the highest form of wisdom, which opens new dimensions to the one enlightened. The manners of meditation and metaphysical accounts of Theravāda and Mahāyāna may differ greatly from one another, but both main forms of Buddhism agree that the highest possible experience achieved in meditation leads to salvation by virtue of the intuitive knowledge it includes.

Buddhist spirituality is a spirituality of salvation, and reflects the universal character of Buddhism as a world religion. The multitude of its forms reveals many human and religious values. We have been able to trace two of the major trends: the existential, practical trend resulting from the nature of Buddhism as a religion of salvation, and the meditative trend leading through cognition to the mystical realm. In concrete life, these trends are not separate but interconnected, offering many points of contact for a dialogue on the essential points of religious life.

Notes

1   On present-day Buddhism's evaluation of original Buddhism see Dumoulin, *Buddhismus der Gegenwart,* index: "Urbuddhismus."

2   Particularly well known is the story of the man hit by a poisoned arrow who wished to know all about his assailant before letting the doctor pull the arrow out of him to save his life. (Majjhimanikāya No. 63).

3   The appellations "Minor Vehicle" (Hīnayāna) and "Major Vehicle" (Mahāyāna) were created by the adherents of the Mahāyāna schools. Today the adherents of the "Minor Vehicle" call their way "the Doctrine of the Elders" (Theravāda). This name, however, pertains only to the parts of this branch of Buddhism still extant today in Ceylon and Southeast Asia.

4   *Jikaku kakuta* (literally "self-enlightenment—enlightenment for others") expresses the same thought as *jiri rita.* Waddell and Abe translate this expression in Dōgen's *Bendōwa* as "the dimension of self-enlightenment qua enlightening others"; and remark in a footnote: "without enlightening others there is no self-enlightenment, and *vice versa.* This is the essence of Mahāyāna Buddhism, realized for Dōgen in *jijuyū samādhi* that includes *tajuyū samādhi.*" See "Dōgen's *Bendōwa.* Translation by Norman Waddell and Abe Masao," *The Eastern Buddhist,* New Series vol. IV, no. 1 (1971), p. 136.

5   On the Sōka-Gakkai movement see Dumoulin, *Buddhismus der Gegenwart,* pp. 166-187.

6   The Pāli canon lists the three good healing roots and the three deleterious evil roots (*māla*). Compare the article "Māla,"

Nyanatiloka, Buddhistisches Wörterbuch (Konstanz, 1952), pp. 129-131. "Ignorance" in this formula is synonymous with *mūmyō,* the Chinese expression for the ignorance that is the first link in the twelve-part chain of causation. See S. Mochizuki, *"sandoku"* in vol. II, p. 1628f. and *"chi"* in vol. IV, p. 3548f. of *Bukkyō Daijiten.*

7   Winston King treats the four Brahma abodes extensively in Chapter III, "Love, Christian and Buddhist," of his book *Buddhism and Christianity,* pp. 64-102. See also the chapter "Buddhist Charity" in Henri de Lubac, *Aspects of Buddhism* (London and New York, 1953), pp. 15-52. Both authors are aware of the differences between the goodwill and compassion praised by the Buddhist scriptures and the Christian love of neighbor.

8   The etymological root of *maitrī* is the same as that of *mitra,* the Sanskrit word for "friend." Cf. *"Jihi,"* *Shin-Bukkyō Jiten* (New Buddhist Encyclopedia), ed. Hajime Nakamura (Tokyo, 1962), p. 241.

9   The relationship between Buddhist compassion and Christian love of neighbor is not derived from any text, but rather rests on particular remarks and expressions which I have heard in personal meetings and conversations. See my account in Chapter II.

10   Cf. Watanabe, *Bukkyō* (Buddhism), Iwanami Shinsho series No. 258 (Tokyo, 1956), pp. 176ff.

11   On repentance and its rites, See Heinrich Dumoulin, "The Consciousness of Guilt and the Practice of Confession in Japanese Buddhism," *Studies in Mysticism and Religion: Festschrift Gershom G. Scholem* (Jerusalem, 1967), pp. 117-129, with bibliography; also S. Dutt, *Early Monastic Buddhism* (Calcutta 1971), and M. W. de Visser, *Ancient Buddhism in Japan,* vol. I (Leiden, 1935).

12   The texts recited at the ceremonies of repentance are in the form of a general confession of all "sins committed by body, speech and mind." Similarly, a prayer named the "Buddhist Common Prayer" by the well-known Burmese Buddhist Pe Maung Tin contains a general confession of sin (cited by Winston King, *op. cit.,* p. 156). Shāntideva, the author of the famous 7th century Indian Buddhist poem *"Bodhicaryāvatāta"* ("Descent into the Course of Awakening") recounts his mistakes in a very personal confession

of "all evils that I have committed." The text is in M. Wintermitz, *Der Mahāyāna-Buddhismus* (Tubingen, 1930), p. 72. And a present-day Zen disciple practiced spontaneous repentance of her faults which reappeared one after the other in her memory. See Dumoulin, "Technique and Personal Devotion in the Zen Exercise," p. 37.

13   On repentance in Zen Buddhism see the brief statement on the teachings of the Sōtō school compiled from the writings of the Zen Master Dōgen called Shushōgi. "Actual repentance" is also called "superficial repentance," in counterdistinction to the "deep repentance" experienced in enlightenment. On the teachings of Shushōgi see the chapter entitled "Der religiöse Heilsweg des Zen-Buddhismus und die christliche Spiritualität," in Dumoulin, *Östliche Meditation und christliche Mystik,* pp. 257-277.

14   Thus Japanese Zen Master Sogaku Harada attributes an ultimate responsibility to human freedom when he writes, "If we deliberately transgress against the way of the *Dharma,* without asking to be awakened to choose the way, then even the great mercy of the Buddhas and the Patriarchs cannot help us." *Shushōgi Kōwa* (Tokyo, 1953), p. 92. Compare also Harada's express repudiation of determinism, pp. 51ff.

15   Compare the "Problem of Sin," *Living Buddhism in Japan. A Report of Interviews with Ten Japanese Buddhist Leaders* (Tokyo, 1960), pp. 31-37. Here various viewpoints are represented, and the social aspects of sin are dealt with. The followers of Amida Buddhism emphasize man's involvement in karma, but express doubts as to the teaching on the cycle of reincarnations and on preexistence. On rites of repentance in Amida Buddhism see Dumoulin, "The Consciousness of Guilt and the Practice of Confession in Japanese Buddhism," pp. 119, 125. The trusting invocation of the Buddha Amida (*nembutsu*) is considered to be extremely effective toward deliverance from sin. Charles Eliot writes that "The recitation of the Nembutsu with faith implies repentance for sin in the past and the desire to avoid it in the future." *Japanese Buddhism* (London, 1930), p. 184.

16   Masaharu Anesaki, *History of Japanese Religion* (London, 1935), p. 370.

17   The word "suffering" does not adequately render the full meaning of the Pāli *dukkha,* which comprises not only every sort of bodily and psychic pain, but also evil in the world and individual existence. In the cycle of rebirth, suffering and impermanance are inextricably linked together.

18   King cites a prayer directed to Gautama which expresses "a sense of sin and guilt, with repentance to follow." *Op. cit.,* p. 111. Improvised prayers are often included in the reports of present-day Zen disciples. Cf. Dumoulin, "Technique and Personal Devotion in the Zen Exercise," pp. 28ff. The practice of repentance and prayer occurs in new, Buddhist-inspired religions as well. See Dumoulin, *Buddhismus der Gegenwart,* pp. 156, 165, 173f.

19   The symbolic art of Amarāvatī particularly expresses this kind of devotion. See the plates in Douglas Barrett, *Sculptures from Amarāvatī in the British Museum* (London, 1954).

20.   From *Tōkyō Honganji-hō* (monthly publication of the Honganji Temple in Asakusa, Tokyo), no. 77 (November 1967).

21   The six ways are the six stages within which living beings transmigrate: the stages of hell, hungry spirits, animals, *asuras,* men, and heaven (*deva*).

22   See Dumoulin, "Buddhismus im modernen Japan," *Buddhismus der Gegenwart,* pp. 140f.

23   Ch. H. Puech, *Le Manichéisme* (Paris, 1949), p. 71, cited in J. A. Cuttat, "Expérience Chrétienne et Spiritualité Orientale," *La Mystique et les Mystiques,* ed. A. Ravier (Paris 1965), p. 901.

24   *Ibid.,* p. 902.

25   J. A. Cuttat, "Östlicher Advent und gnostische Versuchung," *Kairos,* vol. II (1960), pp. 145-163.

26   On meditation in early Indian Buddhism, the so-called Hīnāyana meditation, see A. Bareau, "La Mystique Bouddhiste," *La Mystique et les Mystiques,* pp. 680-690; F. Heiler, *Die buddhistische Versenkung* (Munich, 1918); Dumoulin, "Meditation in The-

ravāda," *Östliche Meditation und christliche Mystik,* pp. 192-201, and the relevant chapters in the general works on Buddhism.

27   *Satipatthāna Sutta;* German translation and commentary by Nyanaponika Thera: *Satipatthāna: Der Heilsweg buddhistischer Geistesschulung* (Konstanz, 1950). See also the two classic treatises on ancient meditation: the Vimuttimagga of Upatissa, English translation from the Chinese by N. R. M. Ehara, Soma Thera and Kheminda Thera (Colombo, 1961); the original Pāli text has not been preserved, and the Chinese version dates from the 6th century A.D. See also the Visuddhimagga of Buddhaghosa, English translation by Bhikkhu Nanamoli (Colombo, 1956).

28   Heiler, for example, points to a similarity between some objects of Christian meditation, i.e. death and transitoriness, and similar topics of Buddhist meditation. *Op. cit.,* p. 16f.

29   This is meditation on the four Brahma-abodes (*brahmavihāra*); see note 7 of this chapter.

30   The most widespread of these is the "new Burmese method of meditation." See Nyanaponika Thera, *Satipatthāna: The Heart of Buddhist Meditation* (Colombo, 1956); Dumoulin, "Exkurs über die neue burmesische Meditationsmethode im Vergleich mit dem Zen-Weg," *Östliche Meditation und christliche Mystik,* pp. 209-216.

31   See Masao Abe, "Zen and Western Thought," *International Philosophical Quarterly,* vol. X, no. 4 (1970), pp. 501-539.

32   Heiler, *op. cit.,* p. 62.

CHAPTER 5

Ultimate Reality and the Personal

The Buddhist way of salvation entails a relationship between man and ultimate reality. We have already examined the existential religious experiences of transcendence and have been able to recognize genuine examples of this kind of experience in many branches of Buddhism. At the same time, however, we noted a particular resistance to theism.

A perfected theism tends toward the personal, in fact summons and incorporates it. Thus the question of an ultimate reality and the quest of the personal belong together—or, to put it another way, to ask whether Buddhism is a theistic religion is ultimately to ask for evidence of personal elements in Buddhism. On its path to salvation Buddhist spirituality gives rise to a number of expressions of piety which point in a theistic direction. A certain tentativeness clings to many of these expressions of Buddhist piety. Still, even such tentative religious activities, insofar as they are genuine and spontaneous, are a part of the Buddhist religion and are essential to our understanding of its totality. As has often been noted, the religion of the Buddha must itself be counted among the non-theistic religions in spite of the theistic tendencies it demonstrates, for in it the nonpersonal is predominant. We are, therefore, all the more concerned with the relation between the non-personal and the personal in Buddhism, and with the question whether there is enough room for the personal in Buddhism to serve as a point of departure for the Buddhist-Christian dialogue.

The Cosmic and the Personal

The cornerstones of ancient Buddhism are the nonpersonal principles of karma and *Dharma*. Karma refers to the principle of the ever-recurrent reprisal of all deeds; it is in continuous effect in the course of continuous reincarnations, regardless of the change in the reincarnated. *Dharma,* meaning duty, law or teachings, is defined as the ground of the path of salvation in the semantic roots of the word: the Sanskrit *dhr* signifies bearing or supporting. In ancient Buddhism, the kinds of meditation we have spoken of as mindfulness and clairvoyance (*sati-vipassanā*) serve to realize the *Dharma*; today this form of meditation is being revived in Theravāda Buddhism. It consists primarily of becoming aware of things and their interrelationships, which is to say the *dharmas,* the elements or components of all existing things. The person meditating mindfully ascertains the *dharmas* and thus gains insight into the *Dharma,* which is expressed above all in the teaching of the Four Holy Truths. But it should be noted that the Buddha embodies the *Dharma* just as the *Dharma* represents the Buddha. This relation between the Buddha and the *Dharma,* heightened to the point of identity, suggests a relation between the non-personal and the personal. For no matter how later Buddhism developed the doctrine of the Buddha, the Buddha-category is never completely severed from its roots in the person Shākyamuni. If the Buddha is found in the *Dharma* and the *Dharma* in the Buddha, then as the Buddha is de-personalized into the notion of the *Dharma* (leading to the teaching of the cosmic or *Dharma*-body of Buddha), so the *Dharma* receives a personal hue through the Buddha.

Mahāyāna Buddhism has perfectly expressed the identity of the Buddha and *Dharma.* The Buddha became the cosmic principle of all reality. The great Mahāyāna sutras speak of this elevation in symbols, while Mahayanistic speculative philosophy reflects on the all-encompassing oneness of reality drawn together in the Buddha. In the Mahāyāna schools, meditation serves to realize this oneness of reality. Here we shall pay more attention to the spiritual meditation than to the ambiguous monistic metaphysics of Mahāyāna. This meditation is also colored by the cosmic, as is clearly shown by the way of enlightenment of Zen Buddhism, representative of the Mahāyāna schools which possess a philosophical foundation.

The significance of Zen meditation derives from the experience of enlightenment, in which the person meditating breaks through to a new dimension, the dimension of perfect unity exclusive of any kind of duality. Zen disciples, in harmony with the cosmic view of Mahāyāna, understand this experience as a non-personal contact with absolute reality, akin to what some Western psychologists have called "cosmic consciousness."[1] Zen Buddhists justify the elimination of the personal from this level of consciousness by the widespread philosophic view that the notion of person necessarily entails a duality and is thus inadmissible in the highest stage of experiencing reality. According to this view, the mystical experience of ultimate reality is not personal because self and cosmos unite to form the ultimate non-personal reality.

But is this philosophical supposition necessary, and is it corroborated by the experience of enlightenment? Are cosmic universality and personal self incompatible?

Perhaps the writings of Teilhard de Chardin can throw light on this matter. In his spiritual view of the world, Teilhard combines a cosmic outlook with a very explicit personalism. At the same time, his spirituality converges with Far Eastern thinking.[2] He was attuned to the all-encompassing continuity of reality just as spiritual leaders of Asia are. We may ask how his cosmic sense of the world relates to his personalistic convictions.

Teilhard speaks of his "Christian cosmic feeling"[3]; he once wrote that his vocation was "to personalize the world in God."[4] For him the cosmos is "a personal Universe" and a "personalizing Universe."[5] He rejects the "widely accepted ideal that the All, even when expressed as Spirit, can only be impersonal."[6] "The Universe," he writes, "is a vast thing, in which we would be lost if it did not converge upon the Person."[7] In his main work on the philosophy of nature, *The Phenomenon of Man,* Teilhard expounds his view that the Universe must develop and form the personal in order to have the capacity to admit man as person. It is true that in his early works he occasionally speaks of depersonalization, dissolution of one's own personality, destruction of the ego and losing oneself in God. But, as Henri de Lubac convincingly argues, such expressions must be understood in the mystical sense: they signify only Teilhard's mystical Christocentrism, which he pinpointed in the phrase "to transfer to 'Christ' the ultimate center of our existence."[8] The *telos* of unity toward which the universe is evolving—one might say converging—is, as Teilhard explicitly notes, not a "shoreless ocean" nor a "diffuse immensity,"[9] but rather something which is "supremely Personal and supremely Personalizing."[10]

Teilhard's view of the universe unites his cosmic feeling for life with his basic personalistic convictions. The idea of a personal cosmos has for him been transposed into flesh and blood. Thus, in a letter where this theme is at first only peripheral, he bases his optimistic belief in goodness, warmth, and love in this world on the profoundly personal character of the world, with a reference to the natural sciences. He writes that "no other faith 'than the Christian' . . . can make this world which surrounds us . . . inwardly warm and friendly to the same extent, for in its end and in its essence, the world is personal, steadfast, and loving. The real threat to mankind is not that the earth should cool, but that the world should become entirely unpersonal and ice-cold. And this, if I am not mistaken, is a strictly biological question of survival."[11]

In Teilhard's thought, the personal and the cosmic do not contradict each other. The personal character of the world has its ground in the personal being of ultimate reality. God is the "supreme pole of personalization, the ultrapersonalizing centre; He is personal and "hyper-personal."[12] Where Teilhard reflects on his faith and explains it to the non-believer, he shows how the path from belief in the world leads through belief in the Spirit, in immortality and in the personal, to belief in a personal God and his revelation in Christ. Man and the ever-converging and personalizing cosmos are evolving toward the supreme personal unity, namely, toward the omega point, Christ.

One can look at Teilhard's view, that all of reality is undergoing a process of personalization, from various points of view, Insofar as it rests on Teilhard's personal intuition, there is no compelling reason to accept it. Yet as it is inspired by a Christian faith, it is not at odds with the teachings of Christianity. This harmony should be stressed, for even some Christians have been critical of Teilhard because of the way his thinking combined the personal and the cosmic. The question whether there are sufficient philosophical-theological reasons for Teilhard's view must remain open here. In the following we shall have occasion to consider two points which might lend evidence in support of the Teilhardian scheme. First, if in the relation between person and being it should prove that being itself can be understood as essentially personal, then it would be possible with Teilhard to discover the personal throughout reality. Further, in the light of a personal divine creation, it would be plausible to see the cosmos as pervaded by the personal. We shall return to these points later.

The Person in the Perspective of History

The concept of history is primarily opposed to that of the cosmos. Whereas the cosmos includes the totality of nature and its course in time, in which man appears as just one strand among many, history as generally understood has man and his actions as its total content. As minuscule as man in nature is, he is able to determine the course of history through his conscious and free decision-making. History is the stage on which man's personal drama is played out. The cosmic realm may threaten to devour the person, but the perspective of history places the person in the immediate foreground. And because the events of history flow from man's own personal nature, person and history both are universally human.

It appears, however, that different peoples and cultures have developed a consciousness of history in different degrees. In general, the Occident from its beginnings has been more historically conscious than the Orient. But again, China stands out in Asia for its historical thinking, while the otherwise highly developed culture of India strikes us as lacking in historical perspective. In the context of our discussion it is to be kept in mind that historical consciousness is closely related to the religious ideas of a people or culture. It is known that an extraordinarily strong and religious sense of history was brought to the fore in Judaeo-Christian tradition. Certain ideas of historical thinking—the beginning and end of defined periods of time, movement toward an end or *telos*, a drama-like unfolding of history, uniqueness of events, and so on—are epitomized in Christianity. For Christianity sees itself as a history of salvation in terms of the Christ-event which is its center, and of the kingdom of God which carries human history toward its eschatological fulfillment. This religious conception springs from a belief in a personal God whose providence, saving action, and gracious redemption enter into human history. Even in the modern secularized view, in which progress and reason take the place of divine providence, the Western philosophy of history remains bound to its origins in Christian theology.[13]

Evidently Asia does not have a conception of history comparable to the religiously inspired Western conception. The enthusiasm of the Chinese for their history is a non-religious one. The classical Chinese picture of history, as far as religion is concerned, has hardly evolved beyond mythical thinking; its force is in the worldly realm. The higher religions of Asia have no intrinsic relation to the historical. Is this absence the consequence of a weak awareness of person, or is consciousness of the person weakly developed because the corresponding historical consciousness is lacking? In any case, the two are closely related.

Buddhism has been depicted as "a non-historical religion."[14] The adherents of this view regard this unhistorical attitude as a main difference from the Christian religion. This difference is especially important in philosophy and metaphysics. As an example there is the *Hua-yen* (Japanese: *Kegon*) school representative of Mahāyāna Buddhism and stemming from the Avatamsaka Sutras. This school has expressed the Easterner's cosmic sense of life more fully than any other. In the prologue to his study of the philosophy of Hua-yen Buddhism, Garma C. G. Chang approaches the difference between "the Buddhist view and that of the Judaeo-Christian tradition" in terms of their differing historical perspectives, and succinctly contrasts the two. In the Buddhist view, there is, Chang stresses, the idea of a plurality of histories in innumerable universes. ". . . By no means is earth the only stage upon which a unique drama, willed by an authoritative God, is performed." The concept of karma is the key to understanding the Buddhist notion of history. All "history, human or otherwise, . . . is brought into being by the collective karma of sentient beings." The pattern of history is determined by the nature of the collective karma of sentient beings in a determinate history.[15]

The idea of karma, like that of reincarnation, was borrowed, adapted and introduced into Buddhist teachings from ancient Indian tradition. It is one of the comprehensive concepts combining Mahāyāna philosophy with the insights of early Buddhism. Karma, which literally means deed or action, is usually explained in terms of cause and effect as the universal law governing the action and consequences of all historical and natural events.[16] Since karma is thought of as an impersonal law, the personal moment in history is not brought to bear in the karmic view of events. The law of karma cannot be seen through by man; as Chang puts it, "The mystery of karma is as imponderable as the mystery of the Will of God."[17] But whereas the mystery of the Will of God, which underlies human history, derives from the personal nature of God, the law of karma is mysterious along the lines of natural laws. It has been compared to Newton's third law of motion, by which every action has an equal and opposite reaction, and applied to the moral aspects of life.[18] Insofar as the Buddhist stance toward history reflects the non-personal character of the karmic law, it is diametrically opposed to the Christian view of history. At this point, the opposing philosophical backgrounds can hardly serve as a point of departure for the interreligious dialogue.

Nevertheless, the idea of karma does not necessarily exclude every type of human initiative in history. Western scholars who equate belief in karma with a kind of historical fatalism go too far. For karma refers to external circumstances surrounding human life and leaves room for a limited freedom of the will. And though the early, strict notion of karma may hardly have been compatible with a progressive view of history,[19] the karmic idea assumed many forms in Buddhism over the centuries. Thus the original teaching of the Buddha, with its exclusive emphasis on individual salvation, its unworldly asceticism and narrow idea of karma, is unfavorable to the idea of history. But Buddhists in all Asiatic countries have still engaged in political and social action. The history of Buddhism recounts many exchanges between this religion and the political life of Asiatic cultures. In Southeast Asian countries, where the monastic order (*Sangha*) ordinarily enjoyed the patronage of the sovereign, Buddhist monks have used their position to influence the politics of the people.[20] In East Asia, the domain of Mahāyāna Buddhism, the Confucian idea that the "public" must be given primacy over the "private" has molded the popular consciousness of history. Here, Buddhism was generally not able to assume an authoritative position in politics or government. Still, Buddhism came to be a part of the national consciousness in Japan, for example, as in the Theravāda countries of South Asia. In fact, the mingling in politics even became a noted characteristic of Japanese Buddhism.[21]

The proximity of Buddhism to the course of political history so evident in various places and ways in the Middle Ages, indicates that the concrete practice of the religion of the Buddha is not so other-worldly as is often claimed. Yet the individual indications are not sufficient for us to assume that we can find in Buddhism a religiously founded and comprehensive historical consciousness. That consciousness is only rudimentary, both in Theravāda and in Mahāyāna Buddhism. True, it disproves the thesis that the idea of history is entirely alien to the Buddhist way of thinking, but from the viewpoint of the Buddhist way of salvation it must be considered peripheral.

In those lands where Buddhism deeply penetrated several social strata, there often evolved a popular consciousness of a kind of mission that extended even to the realm of official politics. Thus, for example, "The Buddhists of Ceylon and Burma are convinced that their nations have a special mission to fulfill."[22] This accounts in part for the fact that these peoples have tried to establish Buddhism as the state religion. Evidently they seek an ideal state in which the fruit of religion is connected to political power and national security. It is true that those who harbor such thoughts cannot base them on the teachings of the Buddha himself, but ever since the reign of the ideal sovereign Ashoka this ideal has been at home in Buddhism.

In Mahāyāna Buddhism there developed messianic expectations known from early Buddhism and connected to the notion of historical epochs. These hopes were generally formulated according to the traditional scheme of the three ages of the true *Dharma* (Japanese: *shōbō*), the merely externally observed *Dharma* (Japanese: *zōbō*), and the final *Dharma* at the end of time (Japanese: *mappō*). Here certainly we have to do with a messianic and eschatological conception, although for Buddhism there is no absolute *eschaton* which concludes world history.

According to the predominant view in Japan, the world-epoch of the Buddha Shākyamuni toward the end of the Heian period entered into the final age. An excitement high with eschatological hopes spread throughout the populace. It was this frame of mind which generally inspired the Buddhist movements of the Kamakura era. Whereas the Amida schools held that the trusting surrender to the Buddha Amida was the only way to salvation from sin and plight, the Nichiren movement for the first time incorporated a kind of political Buddhism on Japanese soil.[23] In the message of Nichiren, an explicitly political function was allocated to the Buddhist religion. If the Japanese people would totally submit to belief in the Lotus Sutra, as Nichiren demanded, then not only would they be saved from the threatening Mongols, but over and above that they would be called to bring about the salvation, in the Buddhist sense of the word, of the entire world. As the elected "Ordination Platform" (Japanese: *kaidan*),[24] Japan would assemble all the peoples of the earth and bring salvation to them through the Lotus Sutra. This messianic consciousness of history—the Buddhist version of the World War II Japanese imperialism inspired by Shintoism—did not prevail, but present day movements in the Japanese Buddhist new religions are still linked to those messianic hopes.[25]

From these few remarks about the history of Buddhism, we may conclude that Buddhists are familiar with the notion and consciousness of history to varying degrees. The mind most open to historical consciousness in the East is that of the Ceylonese and the Japanese. The phenomenon of political Buddhism, encouraged by external circumstances, is a recent one, and its sudden and unexpected success has caused much surprise. But on closer look it appears that the prerequisites for this development have long been in the making. Throughout the increasing influx of Western culture into Asia, Buddhists have had to face problems of society and politics. It was because of this that they came across the question of the relation between person and history which has been a theme of our inquiries. Today

Buddhists feel challenged by the changing times and called upon to make practical decisions and to think through the problems in a new way, in order to include, wherever possible, a renewed Buddhist idea of history in their world-view.

From the point of view of praxis, the achievement of the Japanese new religion Sōka-Gakkai is noteworthy. To be sure, this movement, true to its this-worldly attitude, does not engage in metaphysical questioning, and a theology of history is not to be expected from it. But the political action demanded by its educated members openly furthers consciousness of the person. Moreover, the search for politically effective models has led to a conception of history inspired by Nichirenism and developed by the president of the Sōka-Gakkai, Daisaku Ikeda, in his futuristic vision of the "Third Civilization" (*dai san bummei*). Nevertheless, this new religion can probably succeed in establishing an inner and organic connection between political influence on history and the fundamental religious doctrines of Buddhism even less than did Nichiren, the prophet of the Kamakura era, from whom the Sōka-Gakkai derives.

Theoretical inquiry into history is just beginning in Buddhist circles, but the problem is in sight and questions are being raised. Here I am referring first and foremost to observations of Buddhist friends who have often brought up this matter in conversation; at present I know of no published Buddhist investigation of greater importance. It is difficult to foresee how far Buddhists will be able to include a systematic doctrine of history in their world-view. When man is opened to the totality of existence, history impinges upon ultimate reality. The Buddhist conception of history, if it is to satisfy the demands of religious man, would have to be connected to the Buddhist experience of transcendence.

Mystical Experience and Philosophical Reflection

The questions we shall deal with in this section might be formulated thus: is mystical experience essentially personal or apersonal? Can we discern and distinguish non-personal and personal elements in the mystical experience? Might the apersonal or the personal character of mystical experience reveal something about the character of ultimate reality? How are we to judge whether an experience is personal or non-personal?

Such questions compel us to recall that, according to the unanimous voice of both Eastern and Western mystics, all mystical experience is ineffable. To be sure, mystical phenomena have recently been the subject of thorough psychological investigation ranging from modern experiments to classical mystical literature, predominantly from the West. But with respect to its metaphysical relevance, the mystical remains as full of questions and obscurities as ever. In particular, the enlightenment of Zen—chosen here because it is the best known and most representative mystical phenomenon in the East—stubbornly resists scientific investigation. Ancient Chinese Zen chronicles, profuse in biographical remarks and anecdotal *kōan* stories about early Zen masters, contain no descriptive reports of experience. At the most the characteristic features mentioned in the chronicles intimate the essence of enlightenment. Recently published reports of contemporary Zen disciples who have attained the *satori* experience cannot claim the same authority that the sayings or writings of classical Zen masters possess. The experiences of these reports vary greatly in intensity and value. The judgment of the single experience largely rests on observed effects. It is important to evaluate the indirect criteria carefully, for many people today aim only at sudden and intense psychic stimuli and are satisfied with ephemeral results.

There can be no serious doubt about the authenticity of Zen enlightenment as an experience of reality. If mystical experience is psychologically and phenomenologically an immediate grasp of "the approaching of the all-embracing" in meditative consciousness,[26] the Zen experience clearly fits this description. As we have already noted, reports of the experience of Zen enlightenment show its profound similarity to experiences of cosmic consciousness. The ecstatic character of the lived Zen experience is especially apparent. But other traits of cosmic consciousness, such as the experience of oneness with the universe, the dissolution of the subject-object dichotomy, hyperclarity of vision, all-pervading light, and so on, are also present in Zen enlightenment. Zen disciples often explain, as do many cosmic clairvoyants, that the immediacy of their lived experience is analogous to that of immediate sense perception. Phenomenologically speaking, the experiences of cosmic consciousness border on the pseudomystical and the mystical realm.[27] The experience of an approaching totality or all-comprehensiveness points to a genuinely mystical context. In Zen enlightenment, the "Nothingness" (Japanese: *mu*) already present in meditation and grasped in enlightenment accentuates the absolute character of the experience. In breaking through to Nothingness, all is realized in Nothingness, just as Nothingness is realized in the all. In profound Zen experiences, when the master spurs on the disciple who has had his first deep contact to grasp "the roots of Nothingness," the disciple feels that he is in touch with the ultimate ground of being. It appears that it is precisely the grasp of reality as Nothingness which differentiates Zen enlightenment from the known experiences of cosmic consciousness.

Among genuinely mystical phenomena, "imageless vision" comes closest to Zen enlightenment. In terms of visual perception and imagination, imageless vision is an extreme pole of the process of increasing image-formation. "Imageless vision is insuperably lacking 'in qualification' . . . it is a peering into darkness where nothing is recognized, but present in this darkness is precisely what the person seeks." "He who peers and penetrates into this unmeasurable abyss and is embraced by the dark, unadorned depths, sees nothing of the essence of this abyss, loses himself in the Nothingness of darkness; but from this abysmal darkness the lava of presence glows—and that is what is existentially decisive and motivating." "In imageless vision, nothing is seen."[28] Darkness, depth, abyss, Nothingness—these are the terms (not to be understood in any pessimistic sense) of a mysticism which is especially akin to the mysticism of the Zen way. Its Western representatives are advocates of a *theologia negativa,* stemming from the Pseudo-Dionysius and passed down to Meister Eckhart, to Tauler, Suso and the Fleming, John Ruysbroeck. In the writings of these mystics, speculative thought commingles with genuinely mystical experiences in a way which makes a clear demarcation between the two almost impossible. Experience and reflection are inextricably interwoven. And Zen is uniquely similar to this Western school of "philosophical mysticism" characterized by imageless vision—a fact often noted.

"Every kind of experience necessarily includes a simultaneous interpretation on the part of the experiencing person."[29] If this is true in every case, then not only do sensations first become sense perceptions through the performance of recognizing or interpreting their content, but spiritual intuitions and the broad spectrum of mystical experiences as well are inconceivable without accompanying interpretation. Because they are interpretive and interpretable, they serve as dynamic constituents of man's cultural history. Reflective interpretation does not detract from an experience, but rather makes its context and consequences more clear. One can attempt therefore to locate apersonal and personal dimensions in experience, and find that there are some mystical experiences with no perceived personal elements and others whose structure is not complete without the reference to the personal.[30] The phenomena of cosmic consciousness and of imageless vision reveal no obvious personal dimensions; they seem to be neutral or "it"—experiences, which, if at all, grasp the Absolute in its naked presence, unqualified and unadorned. But other experiences clearly show the personal nature of the Absolute.

Generally speaking, the larger the number of essential characteristics of the experience, the greater is the possibility of deception.[31] Thus personal mystical experiences which are replete with images would be less "certain" than apersonal experiences. Nevertheless, accounts of personal experiences are as numerous and as authentic in the history of mysticism as the apersonal type. Both types can be sufficiently recognized as authentic when the evidence is fully taken into account. The most important criterion for the authenticity of mystical experience is not the "certainty" of their content, but is a function of the total context of the experience and its effects.[32] Mystical experience, which in any case is ineffable, is also to a large extent individual, private, and impossible to duplicate. In spite of the unique character of each mystical experience, the fact that the same type of experience can be observed in almost all cultures at different times, clearly speaks for the genuineness of the mystical grasp of reality.

Is it possible for us to go a step further and discover whether this reality itself is personal or apersonal? Hardly. For our considerations to this point clearly indicate that an experience is ultimately inseparable from its interpretive context. The same fact of experience can receive various phenomenal traits or even meanings according to the varying interpretive contexts. And the experience of grasping the Absolute lends itself to different degrees of consummation. Generally it is the case that we distinguish apersonal and personal mysticism mainly in terms of philosophic or theological world-views in which the experiences in question are embedded. For "no mysticism is merely a heavenly vault. Rather it rests on a foundation which it denies as far as it can, but from which it continuously receives its peculiar character, never identical with forms of mysticism developed elsewhere."[33]

Similarly, Graf Dürckheim, a religious man equally learned in Eastern wisdom and Western psychotherapy, stresses that every culture "interprets experiences of ultimate being according to its own tradition."[34] East and West have gone different ways in interpreting mystical experience. Whereas the East has generally understood the Supreme Being as non-personal, in accordance with Eastern tradition and cultural history, the West has given its spirituality personal dimensions as a result of the influence of Christianity. In Dürckheim's view, the experience of being "always appropriates personal and non-personal components."[35] Experience does not allow one to regard being in itself as non-personal. When the experience is carefully considered from various points of view, it can prove to be open to a personal as well as a non-personal interpretation. This means that the outsider, the one not undergoing the experience, cannot on the basis of the experience alone judge with certainty whether the Supreme and Absolute Being experienced is personal or not.

Discussion of the question of the personal or non-personal nature of reality has led us to philosophic reflection, which in turn is to some degree influenced by the religious world-view of the philosopher. And the place ascribed to any particular experience by a world-view is conditioned by the system of thinking implicit in that world-view itself. Still, it is not the nature of mystical experiences to confirm or to prove a system of thought. Experiences have their own value to the individual, who is encouraged by them on his path to ultimate fulfillment.

Toward the Realm of the Person

We made the point that in itself, experience cannot demonstrate the ultimately personal—or non-personal—nature of transcendent reality. The relation between the personal and the apersonal sphere in the mystical realm has not been sufficiently clarified. With respect to world-views and religions, things at first sight seem somewhat less obscure. The literature in the field has long given the impression that the world-view of the East is nonpersonal, and that of the West personal. Indeed for many, and not without reason, this difference constituted the primary distinction between the world-views of the two hemispheres. Often there were value judgments on both sides accompanying the establishment of this distinction. Here is an obstacle to understanding which threatens the whole enterprise of interreligous dialogue.

To begin with, let us consider two statements which are far removed from any cursory dismissal of "Eastern impersonalism." Graf Dürckheim writes that "in the Easterner's general sense of being as well as in his spirituality, the 'notion of' person does not have the significance which we 'of the West' give it."[36] Further J. A. Cuttat remarks "how alien is the concept of person, as we understand it, to 'the Easterner,' even on the human level."[37] Nevertheless, Cuttat prefers to speak of Eastern spirituality as "pre-personal" rather than nonpersonal, for in his view it does not at all barricade itself from the realm of the personal. We were able to come to a similar conclusion through the relation between the personal and the cosmic in the philosophy of Teilhard de Chardin. If the willingness of the West to discuss with the East a new and more profound understanding of the person is growing, so too Eastern religious men in touch with Western thinking today are paying more attention to this concept. Keiji Nishitani, a leading Japanese Buddhist philosopher, writes that "no doubt . . . the idea of man as a personal being is the highest idea of man which has thus far appeared. The same may be said as regards the idea of God as personal being."[38]

Being a person takes on a special significance in practical life, where one is confronted with responsible moral acts, social reforms, political commitment or a new understanding of history. The efforts at modernization, universal in Buddhism today, have brought about a new appreciation of the personal. One asks, "how can [Buddhism] account for man as 'person' as distinguished from nature?"[39] The concern here is first of all with the actual human being, but we may also note the metaphysical and religious implications of this question. Buddhists now show a notable interest in this problem. Thus, even if we are far from a commonly accepted solution, it is worthwhile to investigate the matter of the personal nature of ultimate reality more thoroughly. In the following I shall attempt some clarification of the problem.

Recently, the Thai monk Buddhadāsa and the Japanese Zen Buddhist Masao Abe—respectively a representative of Southern Theravāda Buddhism and an adherent of Northern Mahāyāna Buddhism—have taken up the theme of Buddhism and Christianity, especially in regard to the question of God. Both have made efforts to understand Christianity, and both acknowledge transcendence and recognize an ultimate reality which Christians call God. Buddhadāsa in fact maintains strongly that "Buddhists also believe in God," and states that "we can say straight away that the concept of God exists also in Buddhism."[40] Masao Abe, on his part, does not call ultimate reality as he understands it God; but the "Absolute Nothingness"—the nucleus of his philosophy—clearly reveals attributes of a Supreme Being. Both these Buddhists concur in denying the notion of a "personal God," for both are faithful to their Buddhist foundations. Abe confesses that, "Frankly speaking, the idea of a personal God is, for Buddhists, one of the most difficult points to understand in Christianity."[41] And Buddhadāsa, after pointing to the notion of God in Buddhism, adds emphatically, but "not of a personal God."[42] The two Buddhists give different reasons for denying a personal God, each according to his particular interpretation of the teachings of the Buddha, and based on his particular metaphysics. But basically the two make the same point, and can be considered representative of Buddhism in general, or even representative of the larger part of Far Eastern spirituality. In the view of the Easterner, the idea of person cannot be applied to the highest form of being, because this idea is anthropomorphic, because it contradicts the absoluteness of Absolute Being, and because it is part and parcel of a belief in creation. These three points deserve clarification.

Person and Anthropomorphism

The naive conception of person as applied to God is anthropomorphic. In ordinary language, the word "person" signifies an individual human being, characterized by such human attributes or abilities as thinking and speaking. The God of the Bible is, to a large measure, described in anthropomorphic terms. The Old Testament God of the covenant is a figure full of human characteristics; he deals with men, becomes angry and punishes, forgives and rewards in a manner thoroughly human. Even in the New Testament, anthropomorphic traits predominate. God appears as Father, King or Shepherd—ideas which psychology and the history of religions long ago established as anthropomorphic. Thus it is not astonishing that the biblical image of God should meet such resistance today. Buddhists, often construing these biblical references literally as the sole Christian idea of God, are forced to reject this overly human and personal god. And in the same spirit they condemn attempts in their own religion which would turn the Buddha into "a personalized center for religious devotion."[43]

In the history of religions, the anthropomorphic idea of God appears as an idea to assist man in his understanding, and reflects a cultural stage in the evolution of man's religious life. Buddhists recognize such aids in their teaching on "skillful means" (Sanskrit: *Upāya,* Japanese: *hōben*). Anthropomorphic representations can correspond to human needs, but must be modified in the course of man's development. This is not a recent discovery, for Christian theology has always been aware of the inadequacy of anthropomorphic elements in man's idea of God. St. Thomas Aquinas' teaching of the *anologia entis* tells us that man is able to speak of God only in terms analogous to human experience. All that can be predicated of God in human speech must be complemented by a radical negation of the finite and an elevation to the unspeakable dimension of the Absolute. This insight, upon which is based all *theologia negativa,* has become of increasing importance in our day. Known since early times in Christianity, this practice of negative predication has been renewed by modern theologians. To name only two examples, Dietrich Bonhoeffer stresses "the ineffability of the name of God," while Karl Rahner mentions "the unspeakable mystery of God." And the recognition of negative theology is no longer confined to theologians and mystics, but has become common knowledge among Christians. It is true that they nevertheless continue to avail themselves of traditional symbols and concepts, but this is right, for these symbols and comparisons mediate truth as it can best be understood by mankind. But at the same time, Christians are more and more aware that all analogies and images referring to God are inadequate, for divine nature is without analogy, imageless, ineffable and full of mystery. This negative theology does not derive simply from the ineffability of mystical experience, but is ultimately grounded in the infinitude of the divine nature itself.

Buddhism has especially incorporated negative theology in two of its forms, namely, in the original Buddhist notion of Nirvāna and in the experience of enlightenment in Mahāyāna Buddhism, especially Zen. The Nirvāna of early Buddhism, according to the description of Winston King as "utterly transcendent," "utterly real," and "utterly desirable,"[44] comes the closest to the Christian idea of God. Corresponding to the description of Nirvāna is the religious, mystical Nirvāna-experience, comprising "the essence of the God-function . . . in Buddhism."[45] In Zen Buddhism as well, the experience of enlightenment is considered unspeakable and utterly real. Its content is usually expressed in the terms of Nāgārjuna's philosophy, whose mystical climax exhibits a negative theology.

We can now proceed one step further and ask whether the Supreme Being grasped through negative theology can also be understood as a personal being. Certainly not, if we equate "personal" with "anthropomorphic." But the matter at hand in no way requires this equation. Negative theology strips the notion of person of all of its anthropomorphic traits, and has done so in Christianity since its beginnings. The personal God was never considered an "ordinary person," but rather was always spoken of "with much qualification."[46] Personal being is absorbed as part of the mystery of God; "the personal dimension of God infinitely transcends human personhood, so that the concept of person, as much as it is illuminating, still proves to be an inadequate similitude."[47] The deepest core of the divine mystery is divine personhood. "If in each of us the ultimate mystery is personhood, then God is the hidden being *par excellence,* for he is the personal being *par excellence.* "[48]

Negative theology corrects the anthropomorphic picture of God. This correction is a prerequisite for any dialogue with the Buddhists, who are thoroughly familiar with negative predication. But this does not mean that religious life should stop with the negative. The "not" of negative theology signifies simultaneously the highest form of affirmation. At a time when European scholars predominantly interpreted Nirvāna as out and out negative, Rudolf Otto discovered the positive jubilation Buddhists experience in Nirvāna. Otto wrote that "Nirvāna is something negative only in concept; in feeling it is something intensely positive, and a *fascinans* which can bring those who enjoy it to rapture."[49] Similarly, in a philosophical context, Masao Abe writes that "Absolute Nothingness in Buddhism is by no means a negative, but an absolutely affirmative principle."[50] Here then are the outlines of a notion of Supreme Being which can be the profitable subject matter of discussion between Buddhists and Christians. And the more the partners base their dialogue on appropriate experiences, the deeper a mutual understanding they will achieve.

The Philosophical Concept of Person

Buddhists also stumble over that philosophical concept of person so fully developed and widely employed in the West. The concept of person is alien to the Buddhist mind. The Buddhists raise the usual objections which we hear in the West, but especially in regard to the application of this concept to Supreme Being they object that "person" in part means limitation and confinement. "If God is a 'person' . . . then it is something finite," Buddhadāsa exclaims and continues to say that no attributes, no form, no characteristics can be predicated of Supreme Being.[51] The misgivings resulting from the common and insufficient notion of person are no doubt justified, and they are recognized in the West as well as in the East. Today we are more than ever aware of the need for clarification of this idea of person.

Dialogue with Eastern philosophers can serve the purpose of clarifying the idea. The so-called Kyoto school of Japanese philosophy, founded by Kitarō Nishida and inspired by Zen Buddhism, has made intense studies of the West's philosophical understanding of person. The present leading exponent of this school, Keiji Nishitani, in an important essay entitled "The Personal and the Impersonal in Religion," makes the point that the Christian notion of a personal God is linked essentially to a teleological world-view, according to which God ordains the course of the universe and guides man and history to a predetermined goal. But, Nishitani continues, modern science has made this world-view questionable. The order of the world, so long taken for granted as the expression of God's personal will, proved to be "unrelated to the personality of God" and "completely controllable by human reason." This newly attained world-view is, according to this philosopher, "incompatible with the idea of 'personality'."[52]

Following Nishitani's negative appraisal is the presentation of his metaphysical convictions, which state among other things that the concept of person is unable to express the perfection of God. Something deeper, more fundamental, something "transpersonal" from which personality derives, must precede this concept.

He speaks of a "personal impersonality;"[53] for the impersonal is, for him, the ultimate and the foundational.

This appraisal rests on a pre-judgment. Why has this Japanese philosopher judged the matter in this way? First we may assume that he is profoundly influenced by Eastern tradition and values, shaped in Zen Buddhism by the Mahayanistic philosophy of Nāgārjuna. The viewpoint concealed in Nishitani's judgment is that of "Absolute Nothingness" which transcends all forms of being, including the personal form. This is Nishitani's philosophical option, and we must grant it to him. To the degree that a philosophy rests on an option, such pre-judgments are carried over into its fundamental insights.

Nevertheless, Nishitani's critique of a personal God raises another point, directly aimed at Western thinking. As a personal being, he states, God must have an opposite as the object of his will and election. Thus, the concept of person necessarily entails a duality. Masao Abe, whose roots are also in the Kyoto school, employs the same argument. He finds his conviction verified in the Christian theology of the Trinity. "In Christianity there is still a distinction of oneself and another, the begetter and the begotten . . . So long as dichotomy and distinction remain, God cannot be the true Absolute . . ."[54] We can answer, however, that Christian theology teaches the indivisible and undivided unity of the Supreme Being and, without diminishing to the three "Persons" of the Divine Mystery, explicitly rejects any dualism in God. This is, of course, not the place for an analysis of Christian theology of the Trinity.

The Buddhist viewpoint takes the unity of the Absolute in a way which relegates the person to a lesser reality than the supreme, perfect unity. Buddhadāsa

states, without further explanation, that the idea of a
personal God requires "another being."[55] We have mentioned that in Nishitani's metaphysics, Absolute Nothingness—which is a "living Nothingness"—stands behind the person. Personality is "a mask of Absolute
Nothingness." Absolute Nothingness is absolute self-
hood and, in absolute non-duality, the ground of personal being.[56] Abe speaks of "the open *topos* of the
Absolute Nothingness where all relative things may
perform their relative roles each retaining its own par-
ticularity."[57] This last quotation leads back to the starting point of our debate. There we saw that the philosophical critique of the concept of person proceeds from
the supposition that being a person entails a limitation
and particularization of being.

Yet the relationship between being and person can
be understood in a way which does not confine the
concept of person to this category. Being itself can be
understood as fundamentally personal. In this view,
person and the transcendent ground of being are equally
transobjective and indivisibly one. This conception of
personal being seems to be as suited to Western thinking
as the foundation of Absolute Nothingness is to Eastern
thought. It appears that the basic experience of being
is interpreted differently, according to its historical and
cultural context. In the Occident, an interpretation of
personal being has formed under the influence of Christianity, and today is the object of renewed reflection.
J. B. Lotz summarizes the basic tenets of a personalistic
philosophy of being as follows: "Being is intrinsically
personal, and for that reason only persons possess being
in the full sense, whereas things participate in being to
a lesser degree. Consequently, the person forms the
nucleus and the goal of reality . . ."[58]

In personalistic philosophy, the phenomenological

method becomes a personological method. Philosophers of this school interpret the experience of being as a personal "I-Thou" experience, and on the grounds of the finite Thou experience they postulate an infinite and absolute Thou. Of course we must keep in mind that the "I-Thou" experience does not constitute the underlying being of the person. But the underlying person is in principle open to communication. The absolute Supreme Being possessing this openness is infinite person, infinite Thou, toward which finite persons ultimately transcend themselves. We cannot deny the value of such an ontological hermeneutic, which interprets reality in terms of personal being. In its view, the transcendent ground of all beings does not lie behind the person, but rather is itself personal: being means being a person.[59]

We have already shown that meditative-mystical experience can be seen from different viewpoints and that no single view can be considered adequate or true by itself. In experience J. B. Lotz finds both "monistic and theistic content." In the monistic version, "the overwhelming and unspeakably felicitous experience of unity with being or with the Absolute" is developed further "toward identity of selfness." Man "intimates . . . his being as a manner of the divine being." On the other hand, in the theistic-personalistic interpretation, man knows that "he stands in relation to being only as participant." He experiences his "being as a way to partake of subsisting being . . ." Lotz stresses that transcendence and immanence are in no way to be separated from each other, "for they essentially interpenetrate." In the end, Lotz considers the theistic-personal interpretation as the more appropriate, since it is "an explication intrinsic to the great experience, and not just a consequential theoretical interpretation." Thus the thorough presentation of the personalistic standpoint by Lotz offers not only an important theoretical contribution, but also new points of departure for the dialogue between East and West.[60]

The Creator-God

The idea of person is linked to the belief in a Creator-God. Buddhists reject this belief and repudiate the anthropomorphism they see in the Christian teachings on creation. Anthropomorphism is especially evident, they maintain, through the mythical character of the creation account of Genesis. The Buddhist religion has no myths of creation,[61] and it was not the least deed of Shākyamuni to clear Vedic mythology and Brahmanistic ritualism out of his religion. In place of belief in creation, Buddhism teaches insight into the twelve-part chain of causation. The causality of this chain is not that of a cause and effect relation, but rather signifies the mutual dependence of all things in their origination. The question regarding the origin of the universe is not the concern; instead existing things are accounted for in the fact of their being, with emphasis on the suffering of the human condition.

Nowhere in its religious teachings has Buddhism sought the cause or origin of the world. The question of the eternity and infinity of the world belongs to those metaphysical questions which Shākyamuni refused to consider. And in the entire course of the history of Buddhism, no doctrine of creation has been put forth. If theistic tendencies began to operate in Buddhology, and Buddha-figures such as Amitābha or Vairocana or even the Shākyamauni of the Lotus Sutras—elevated to the eternal, cosmic Buddha—accentuated the transcendence and the God-function of the Buddha, nevertheless at no time was a Buddha made into a Creator-God. Among the ten honorary titles of a Buddha neither the title of creator nor the name of father so often connected with it is to be found. The Buddha, for his disciples, is the Enlightened One, the Sublime, the Holy, the One worthy of veneration; he is called the teacher of the *devas* and of men, occasionally Lord of the world as well, but never creator. Creation myths of autochthonic religions which Buddhism came into contact with and accommodated, always remained peripheral. Never was a belief in creation integrated into the teachings of Buddhism.

In the encounter with Christianity, Buddhists like to propose the teaching on the Creator-God, so unacceptable to them, as the main line of demarcation. Buddhadāsa is alarmed precisely at the humanized idea of God that he notes in the Genesis account. This "God who created the world," he writes, "had the characteristics of a person, the feelings and thoughts of a person."[62] In order to preserve the sublimity of the divine being, he devotes several pages to interpreting in what he calls a dharmic sense the Old Testament creation account.[63] The God "so mysterious a power, beyond the description of the human tongue,"[64] would have degraded himself in creating the visible world. "A true God should be concerned with the creation of the inner world within human consciousness to deserve the title of God. Had he been busy with the creation of the material world or of a world of flesh, he would have degraded himself to an absolutely meaningless God."[65]

Buddhadāsa's objections to the Christian belief in creation are repeated throughout Buddhism. Insofar as they touch upon biblical anthropomorphism and the forms of Christian belief derived from it, what we have said previously about anthropomorphism holds true. The ineffable mystery of God, which is the center of negative theology, includes creation. Both creation and God in his essence are mysteries. "It is as impossible for man to grasp adequately the activity of God the Creator as it is for man to grasp God Himself, for the creative activity is identified with the Creator."[66] The mystery of creation can easily be obscured in the Christian mind when one accentuates the causal relation between God and his creatures. If one is to speak philosophically of God as the first cause (*causa prima*), then it must be kept in mind that the concept of cause, like the concept of being, is predicated of God and of other beings analogically. That means that the manner in which God acts causally is radically different from any worldly causation. All examples taken from the human realm in order to illustrate divine creation are necessarily inadequate. Such comparisons as that between God and the craftsman, the carpenter or the artist are likely to mislead, since they reduce divine works to human activities. God is not a cause in a human or worldly way, not even as the cosmological cause of the world at the beginning of time or the first in the infinite chain of causes in this world. Rather, God is absolutely other and unique in his activity and in his being.

Christian theology, in interpreting the Genesis account, has always been aware of the special character of that creative activity which is a creation through the Word. In theological terms, "the basic category of the creation doctrine is the Word . . . the concept of causality seems less suited to describe what is meant by creation."[67] The creation doctrine bespeaks "the reference of all being to the *Logos,* to the Word and thus to the spiritually meaningful."[68] In this way the spiritual receives strong emphasis in the creation doctrine. God, so to speak, does not soil his hands by creating the material world. He does not exert himself like a demiurge in giving form to matter. His transcendence over the world remains intact. The rich teaching on creation through the Word is also closely connected to such central Christian truths as the Incarnation and the Trinity. Here we can point out two consequences of this teaching which are of significance for the Buddhist-Christian dialogue.

Christian tradition, in dealing with the doctrine of creation through the Word, has spoken of *creatio ex nihilo*.[69] By this Christians stress God as the ground and cause of all created things. God's creative Word reaches to the very being of things. By gratuitously naming all things, he releases the world into being. Since nothing exists without his Word, he creates—as the phrase goes—out of nothing. Buddhists, in particular Japanese Zen Buddhists, show an active interest in this Christian formulation, in which there appears the word "nothing," so familiar and important to them. They like to compare the creation "out of nothing" with the Nothingness of their own metaphysics. Masao Abe, very much in keeping with classical Christian theology, writes that the "nothing" in the expression *"creatio ex nihilo"* signifies the lack of any preexistent matter and distinguishes the Christian concept of creation from that of Greek philosophy. He goes on to say that this "nothing" is not the dialectical opposite of being, but simply the non-presence of any beings. Creation demonstrates "the Christian belief in the absolute transcendence of God . . . that God's power of being is above any kind of *nihil*."[70] Still, as Abe explicitly points out, the Nothingness of Buddhist metaphysics is carried to an even more profound level, to the "Absolute Nothingness" wherein both being and non-being are grounded, where all differentiation ceases and no duality remains. The strongest objection of Zen Buddhists to the Christian view concerns duality, and we cannot overlook the basic differences in this respect between the Buddhist and the Christian positions. The ideal of unity the Christians have in mind is, as Joseph Ratzinger rightly comments, "a duality in unity, or better: a duality of a unity (of origin) proceeding to a unity (of love)."[71]

The creative activity manifested in creation through the Word proves to be God's personal doing. A personal relation is intrinsic to the Word, because in its essence it reveals the person. In speaking of the Word of God, we must of course pay attention to the ontological dimension of language. God's Word is infinitely different from man's word. The Word of God is saturated with the ineffable mystery of God, but it manifests this mystery as that of divine personhood. When the creation of the world through the Word is proclaimed, all created beings are referred to their origin in a personal God. For that reason, divine personhood is reflected in all of creation. From this perspective of personal creation Michael Schmaus sees the real foundation of Teilhard's thesis of a personalizing universe. "The transcendence from which the world comes is of personal character . . . If reality is a reflection of the personal transcendence which embraces and sustains it, and is real precisely therein, then we cannot avoid ascribing personal traits to [that reality]."[72] This personal character must thus penetrate every creature, and the whole material world, for it too was created by God through his Word. Schmaus stresses the "essential difference or discontinuity" between the world of things and mankind, which he sees grounded in the "differentiation of the personal," i.e., the different degrees of participation in personal being.[73] Nevertheless, this differentiation must not obscure what is held in common. "The common factor consists in the creatureliness of all beings. But this creatureliness as a consequence of the origin of every created being in a personal God, implies some mode of personality."[74]

With respect to creation and God the Creator, the Buddhist-Christian dialogue has much to gain in depth and mutual understanding, so long as it looks at the biblical passages more as an expression of religious faith than as a philosophical, ontological, or cosmological position. Masao Abe, inspired by the theology of Karl Barth, stresses that the Christian doctrine of creation is to be taken in a Christological sense. In a famous passage, Barth says that creation is the extrinsic *raison d'être* of the Covenant, and the Covenant is the intrinsic *raison d'être* of creation. And since the Covenant between Yahweh and Israel attested to in the Bible has its fulfilment in Christ, this means that creation through the Word too is directed toward Christ. Karl Rahner bases the Christological interpretation of creation on a "theological anthropology" in which "man is what is actually intended in creation, as the condition for God's impartation of himself." Rahner concludes that "a theological doctrine of creation must be ordered toward Christology."[75]

The Christological link between creation and redemption is expressed by the two basic connotations of the Word and of love. Belief in Christ as the incarnated Word of God implies belief in creation and redemption effected through this Word. And the force behind the works of creation and redemption is the one and same divine love made visible in the creation of the world and in redemption through Christ. "The Christian faith in God the Creator is not direct but mediated by one's faith in the redemption accomplished by Jesus Christ through his suffering on the cross," Abe writes in the Barthian tradition. "God the Father of Jesus Christ is thus believed to have created the world through the same Love which was at work in the incarnation of his *Logos* for the redemption of man."[76] The Barthian view accentuates the unity of the divine work centered in Christ. Judaeo-Christian tradition, especially orthodox Judaism, pays particular attention to other aspects in the interpretation of the biblical account of creation. This is not the place to explicate Barth's theology of creation in detail, but we are grateful when Buddhists today delve so thoroughly into the best works of modern Christian theology.

It is perhaps characteristic of the Far Eastern mind to see the divine being not as an ever remote transcendence, in the manner of Greek philosophy, but rather as vitally near world and man. Abe, proceeding from Barth's Christological theology, extends the idea of the *kenosis* or emptying of Christ (Phil. II, 7f.) to God the Creator, and sees a kind of divine self-emptying in his creative work. The impelling force, as Abe sees it, is God's love; but thereby God assumes a negativity. Thus, "the Christian God should not be understood as a God aloof from non-being and negativity, but as taking on non-being and negating himself of his own free will . . . Because of his love, God, self-sufficient though he is, negates himself and creates the world which is different from himself."[77] Since this self-renunciation is grounded in the divine essence, namely in God's *agape,* it precedes the self-renunciation of God in the act of creation. Self-renunciation, Abe concludes, is not a motive external to God, but rather is of his very essence.

The self-emptying of God is taken up by Nishitani in a different context. He likewise mentions the *kenosis* passage, and finds the basis of this Pauline expression

of Christ's self-emptying love in the *agape* of the Father
in heaven, who "causes his sun to rise on bad men as
well as good, and his rain to fall on honest and dishonest
men alike." (Matt. V, 45). Nishitani is deeply moved
by this passage from the Sermon on the Mount; and
from this non-discriminating love of the Father, which
"embraces all things in their most concrete form,"[78] he
concludes that "also within God himself is included the
meaning of 'having made himself empty.' "[79] "In the
case of the Son Christ," Nishitani goes on, "this 'selfless
love' is a work which has been fulfilled; in the case of
the Father, it is his original nature."[80] To the selflessness
of a God "who has emptied himself," there corresponds
the Buddhist concept of "Emptiness" (*sūnyatā*). Just as
the self-emptying and the forgiving and redemptive love
of God are linked together in the Sermon on the Mount
and demand of man the most radical love of neighbor
and even of enemy, so too in Buddhism, as Nishitani
goes on to show, Emptiness is the basis of the great
compassion of the Buddha, and the latter serves as the
norm for all inter-human behavior.

Christian theology sees in the *kenosis* passage the
Pauline interpretation of the mystery of Christ, his Incarnation and his way through suffering and crucifixion
to Resurrection. It does not speak of God as having
emptied himself in the strict sense, but rather of the
deposit of God's gift of love, which is always first, which
creates man and the world and has mercy on the sinner.
The interpretation of the Johannine texts by the Church
Fathers (e.g., Origen and Augustine) stresses the *agape*
of the divine essence. The pietistic variety of Protestant
devotion sometimes calls the deposit of God's love in
the act of creation a "condescension," a "humiliation,"
or a "servitude."[81]

A certain similarity of motivation between such expressions and the thinking of Japanese Buddhists may be apparent. Classical Christian theology has not made use of such terms for the reason that they easily lead to an undesirable humanization of God. Yet the important biblical motifs which make present to man the living God in his unfathomable love cannot simply be dismissed as anthropomorphisms. The ineffable mystery of God can be as little grasped through philosophical concepts like immutability, infinitude, eternity, and transcendence as through purely symbolic speech. Whoever is aware of negative theology can make use even of expressions not proper to divinity in order to gain knowledge of God. The Japanese Buddhists discover treasures in the Bible which remain concealed to many Christians. The truth of the self-emptying manifest in the person and the redemptive suffering of Christ can be extended to the essence of God insofar as Christ himself makes the Father visible and reflects the divine essence. Are not the Buddhists who weigh this truth of biblical revelation unconsciously attracted by the mystery of the personal? For self-emptying in the understanding of Scripture demonstrates love, and love is the deepest core of the person of God.

When we turn to the theme of ultimate reality in our dialogue, we know more than ever that circumspection is called for. Logical argument is not proper here, nor are any quick solutions apparent. It is possible, however, to realize in the dialogue two prerequisites for a deeper penetration into truth and for increased mutual understanding. These prerequisites are essential to avoid prejudices which forever bar the way. First we can ask why it is that the other side regards its own position as by far the better and so adamantly clings to it. That is, we Christians can attempt to understand the reasons that the notion of person is so remote from Orientals, while they certainly do not lack a sense of devotion and religious quest. And the Oriental can earnestly ask himself why his Western brother considers the person not only the highest of earthly things, but even the deepest core of the reality he calls God. In weighing the answers to these questions, both partners may be opened to new regions of knowledge. It is to this goal that the modest essay here presented is dedicated.

The second prerequisite aims at undoing any false certainty or self-contentment on either side. Even if the Christian who believes in a personal God rightly grasps a most precious truth, still he can never exhaust this truth, nor even express it adequately in words. In spite of his closeness to the personal God, he journeys as a stranger through unknown lands. And when he nevertheless acts as if he could at any time pull the concept of person out of his pocket and reveal its meaning, thanks to the glorious two thousand-year-old tradition of the West, he should not be surprised at the quiet smile of his Oriental brother. No, the Westerner does not see through the essence of being a person. And what of the Easterner? Are not all of his experiences imperfect, even if in a moment of ecstasy he seems to be transported to a higher dimension? A mere glance at the condition of this world should convince him of the ineptitude of all human efforts to establish a paradise on earth, no matter in what guise it be striven for. Has not that anxiety, which some philosophers believe constitutes the primary mode of human existence, gripped the whole world in unforeseen ways? Where is there a ray of hope for man? Are we not pilgrims underway to the eternal, in quest of ultimate reality? Have we not to assist and learn from each other on the way?

Notes

1　　Compare R. M. Bucke, *Cosmic Consciousness* (Philadelphia, 1901) and also its significance for mysticism in William James, *The Varieties of Religious Experience* (New York–London, 1902). On cosmic consciousness in Zen experience, see H. Dumoulin, "The Zen Experience according to Modern Japanese Accounts," *Studia Missionalia,* vol. XVII (1968), pp. 233ff.

2　　See W. Kunz, "Das Denken des fernen Ostens in der Sicht Teilhard de Chardins," *Perspektiven der Zukunft* (Gesellschaft der Freunde Teilhard de Chardins, Freiburg) vol. I (1967), pp. 4-8; also Dumoulin, *Östliche Meditation und christliche Mystik,* pp. 161-164, where Teilhard's "L'Apport spirituel de l'Extrême Orient" (*Monumenta Nipponica,* vol. XII (1956), p. 10) is cited. This article first appeared in the *Journal for Jewish Thought,* October 1950, (Paris).

3　　In a letter dated 9 October 1916, cited in Henri de Lubac, *The Religion of Teilhard de Chardin* (London, 1967), p. 143. In a chapter on personalism (pp. 143-151), de Lubac has compiled a number of quotations relevant to the theme of person and cosmos. See also the pertinent information by de Lubac in *Blondel et Teilhard de Chardin, Correspondance commentée* (Paris, 1965).

4　　In a letter to a friend, 1917, quoted by de Lubac, *op. cit.,* p. 145. In a letter dated 23 September 1934, Teilhard speaks of his "belief in the ever-growing personality of the world" (p. 146); and in a letter of 6 July 1934, he writes that "In my view, the Personal is again dominating the whole evolution of things." See de Lubac, *op. cit.,* 328, note 23.

5　　"Cosmic life," edited in de Lubac, *op. cit.,* p. 145.

6　　*Comment je crois,* cited in de Lubac, *op. cit.,* p. 150. Teilhard disputes those who would recognize a "principle," a "law," or even a "mystery of nature" or "ultimate spirit of the universe," but in all cases shun calling this something "God." See de Lubac, *op. cit.,* p. 147.

7　　From a letter dated 15 November 1935, cited in de Lubac, *op. cit.,* p. 146.

8   From his first memorandum to Auguste Valensin, dated 12 December 1919; cf. *Blondel et Teilhard de Chardin, Correspondance commentée.* There Teilhard remarks how "the ultimate completion of the world comes about only through a death." In his commentary on this text, de Lubac deals in detail with the significance in mysticism of self-dissolution and of losing oneself. De Lubac clarifies the mystical sense of "de-personalization" in Teilhard, *op. cit.*, p. 148.

9   "Sketch of a Personal Universe," cited in de Lubac, *op. cit.*, p. 147.

10   *Comment je crois,* cited in de Lubac, p. 146.

11   From a letter to an American correspondent (1948), cited in *Informations Catholiques Internationales,* no. 399 (January 1972), p. 17.

12   Cf. the commentary on *Le phénomène humain,* de Lubac, *op. cit.*, p. 146.

13   See the pertinent literature on history, historicity, and salvation-history. Of the numerous works we can here mention only the following: J. Daniélou, *Le mystère du salut des nations* (Paris, 1958); R. G. Collingwood, *The Idea of History* (Oxford, 1946); H. Butterfield, *Christianity and History* (London, 1947); W. Kamlah, *Christentum und Geschichtlichkeit* (Stuttgart, 1951). The Judaeo-Christian theological conception of history was carried over into modern thought, in a secularized form, by Hegel and Marx.

14   Paul Tillich and Arnold Toynbee have been seen as representing this view; cf. C. G. Chang, *The Buddhist Teaching of Totality: The Philosophy of Hua Yen Buddhism* (University Park, Pa., and London, 1971), p. xiv. Chang characterizes the Buddhist notion as "trans-historical," not "non-historical."

15   *Ibid.,* p. xiv. H. Bechert, *Buddhismus, Staat und Gesellschaft* I (Frankfurt–Berlin, 1966), p. 407, is of the opinion that the teaching of a "general or collective karma" was introduced by modern Buddhists and is not found among the teachings of ancient Buddhism. But his term (Japanese *gūgō*) is found throughout Chinese-Japanese Buddhist lexica in the meaning of general social

karma as opposed to individual karma. See for example Hajime Nakamura, ed, *Shin-Bukkyō Jiten* (Tokyo, 1962), p. 156. E. Soothill and L. Hodous, *A Dictionary of Chinese Buddhist Terms* (London, 1937), p. 203, define the terms as "deeds of the community, or even of the individual in their effects on the community." The Chinese-Japanese characters for *gūgō* appear in several passages of the Buddhist canon; cf. S. Mochizuki *Bukkyō Daijiten I* (Tokyo, 1968), p. 643. In his commentary on Abhidharmakosha, H. Sakurabe suggests the expression *sādhārana-karman* as the Sanskrit equivalent of the term; see *Kusharon no Kenkyū* (Tokyo, 1969), p. 386 and index 4. Modern Japanese Buddhists consider the distinction between individual and collective karma inappropriate because, as they believe, "Buddhism takes the position that man finds himself in a mutual relationship of one to all. Collective karma involves the non-collective karma and the latter includes the former." Cf. *Living Buddhism in Japan,* ed. Y. Tamura and W. P. Woodard (Tokyo 1965), p. 84; see also pp. 13f., 33ff.

16   Cf. Christmas Humphreys' description of karma in *Buddhism* (Penguin Books, Harmondsworth, 1951), p. 100. Accounts usually accentuate the character of summation and the effects carried through the generations. Cf. Hajime Nakamura, ed., *Shin-Bukkyō Jiten,* p. 156; also the pertinent Buddhist lexica, *passim.*

17   Chang, *op. cit.,* p. xxv.

18   Humphreys, *op. cit.,* p. 100.

19   Bechert, *op. cit.,* p. 40, deals extensively with the discussions on karma within the current of "Buddhist modernism" and Theravāda Buddhism. The Theravāda Buddhists striving for renewal "conflicted with the idea of karma. This idea is hardly able to help one found a political and social dynamism. Precisely for this reason, the notion of history utilized in the main political and social currents of the Buddhist renewal movement deviates so obviously from traditional Buddhist views."

20   Cf. the passages on the political activities of Buddhist monks in connection with the phenomenon of "Buddhism as a religion of the state" in Bechert, *op. cit.,* p. 23-25.

21   S. Watanabe, in *Japanese Buddhism, A Critical Appraisal,*

(Tokyo, 1970), pp. 38ff, notes that Buddhism in Japan was closely connected to the ruling classes from its beginnings. He finds that nationalism is characteristic of Japanese Buddhism, and gives an extensive account of the minglings of Buddhist monks in politics during the various periods of Japanese history.

22   *Ibid.,* p. 27.

23   There were political monks in earlier periods, but Nichiren was the first Japanese Buddhist to formulate religious-political objectives. Several modern Buddhist movements in different Asian countries have political goals; one can reasonably speak of a "political Buddhism."

24   Similar to the ancient Buddhist *sīmā,* "which means literally boundary, signifies a plot of ground within which Uposatha meetings, ordinations and other ceremonies can take place." C. Eliot, *Hinduism and Buddhism,* vol. III (London, 1921), p. 59.

25   Cf. Dumoulin, "Politischer Buddhismus: Sōka-Gakkai," *Buddhismus der Gegenwart,* pp. 166-187.

26   Thus Carl Albrecht defines mystical experience in his *Psychologie der Mystik* (Bremen, 1951), p. 254. Here we note some of Albrecht's penetrating views based on experience, contained in a sequel, *Das mystische Erkennen* (Bremen, 1958).

27   Albrecht, *Das mystische Erkennen,* p. 37. See the entire section on cosmic consciousness, *ibid.,* pp. 37-49. Albrecht remarks that "Zen Buddhism speaks of a mystical experience which seems to have many structures in common with the experience of 'cosmic consciousness,' " p. 48.

28   Albrecht describes the processes of increasing and decreasing image-formation in terms of the "spectrum of mystical vision" bounded by the two poles of vision (image and imageless vision). Quotations are from *Das mystische Erkennen,* pp. 208, 207, 220.

29   *Ibid.,* p. 237.

30   "There is a non-personal and a personal mysticism. In the first kind, one encounters the comprehensive without recognizing any essential personal structure in it. All Christian mysticism, but not only it, is personal mysticism. . ." Thus distinguishing be-

tween these two kinds, Albrecht goes on to ask whether "the 'He' (as opposed to the 'It') in the mystical encounter can be experienced or even intuited, or whether it always and everywhere remains an interpretive and conceptual category." *Ibid.,* p. 196. Albrecht deals extensively with "the personal structure of the all-comprehensive" on pp. 236-245.

31   Compare the section on "Deception and Error in Mystical Experience" in Albrecht, *Das mystische Erkennen,* pp. 272-300. Albrecht draws up a "gnoseological pyramid" of the degrees of certainty in mystical experiences, and notes that personal mysticism rests on experiences particularly amenable to the dangers of deception. "The series of experiences with increasing personal content corresponds to a series of increasing danger of deception." *Ibid.,* p. 303.

32   *Ibid.,* p. 304. By virtue of this criterion, Albrecht ascribes great significance to personal mystical experiences.

33   Rudolf Otto in his Foreword to S. Ohasama & A. Faust, *Zen—Der lebendige Buddhismus in Japan* (Gotha-Stuttgart, 1925), p. ix.

34   Karlfried Graf von Dürckheim, *Durchbruch zum Wesen* (Zurich, 1954), p. 208.

35   *Ibid.,* p. 209f.

36   Karlfried Graf von Dürckheim, "Psychotherapie, Initiation, Glaube," in W. Bitter, ed., *Abendländische Therapie und östliche Weisheit* (Stuttgart, 1967), p. 36. Evaluations are given by H. Rzepkowski, *Das Menschenbild bei Daisetz Teitaro Suzuki* (St. Augustine, 1971), pp. 51ff.

37   J. A. Cuttat, "Experience Chrétienne et Spiritualité Orientale," in A. Ravier, ed., *La Mystique et les mystiques* (Paris, 1965), p. 875.

38   Keiji Nishitani, "The Personal and the Impersonal in Religion," *The Eastern Buddhist,* vol. III, no. 2 (1970), p. 80.

39   Masao Abe, "Buddhism and Christianity as a Problem of Today," *Japanese Religions,* vol. III, no. 3 (1963), p. 29. Paul Tillich observed a desire for democracy in Japan, but at the same

time noted that both in Japanese Buddhism and in Shintoism, one of democracy's essential prerequisites is missing—the evaluation of every human as a person. See his *Christianity and the Encounter of the World Religions* (New York, 1962).

40   Bhikkhu Buddhadāsa Indapanno, *Christianity and Buddhism* (Bangkok, 1967), p. 9; *Dhamma—The World's Saviour* (Bangkok, n.d.), p. 11.

41   Masao Abe, "Reply to the Debate on Christianity and Buddhism," *Japanese Religions,* vol. IV, no. 2 (1966), p. 56.

42   Cf. Buddhadāsa, *Dhamma—The World's Saviour,* p. 14; further p. 15ff.: "By God we must mean an impersonal God. If God is a personal God, who acts and appears like human beings, capable of getting angry and so forth, then we cannot accept him."

43   Although the Buddha, through his teaching and his image in Buddhism, acquired "the quality of a personalized center for religious devotion," as Winston King points out (*op. cit.,* p. 52), nevertheless Buddhists of all schools have consistently rejected the idea of a personal God.

44   King, *op. cit.,* p. 46-50.

45   "Nirvāna is, functionally speaking, the God-equivalent in Buddhism. . . Therefore, in the end the Buddha becomes functionally and actually a savior God for many rank-and-file Buddhists." King, *op. cit.,* pp. 57, 52. The function of God in Buddhism, according to King, is divided into four central ideas: *Dharma,* karma, Buddha, and Nirvāna. See the chapter "God in Four Parts," pp. 34-63.

46   W. H. Collins and I. T. Ramsey, "A Symposium on Christianity and Buddhism—A Reply to Professor Abe," *Japanese Religions,* vol. IV, no. 1 (1964), p. 35 and vol. VI, no. 2 (1966), p. 7.

47   Joseph Ratzinger, *op. cit.,* p. 141. For Ratzinger, the paradox of the biblical faith in God consists in that "Being is believed to be a person, and person to be being itself; that only the hidden is believed to be He who is most near, only the inaccessible to be he who is accessible; that the One is believed to be He who is this person, who is for all and for whom all are" (p. 102). To what extent this hermeneutic is justified by the scriptural texts them-

selves remains an open question. But the philosophical view of this interpretation reveals the innermost core of Christian-inspired Western thinking.

48   H. de Lubac, quoted in Cuttat, *op. cit.,* p. 874.

49   Rudolf Otto, *Das Heilige* (Gotha, 1929), p. 53.

50   Masao Abe, "Buddhism and Christianity as a Problem of Today," p. 21.

51   Buddhadāsa, *Christianity and Buddhism,* p. 74. He further writes that "God, in the religious language of Buddhism, is neither a person, nor spirit, nor body alone, nor is it body and mind together. But it is nature which is impersonal, devoid of any self. It has no attributes, has no form or size . . . God has no characteristic by which we may say God is like this or like that" (p. 80).

52   Keiji Nishitani, "The Personal and the Impersonal in Religion," p. 13.

53   *Ibid.,* p. 17. Nishitani also speaks of "a kind of transpersonality." Paul Tillich writes that "the *'esse ipsum'* ('being itself') of the classical Christian doctrine of God is a trans-personal category which makes it easier for the Christian partner of the dialogue to understand the meaning of the 'Absolute Nothingness' of Buddhist thought. . . . In Mahāyāna Buddhism, the spirit of the Buddha appears in many manifestations endowed with personal qualities, and thereby facilitates a non-mystical, often very primitive relationship with the divine being . . ." (*op. cit.,* p. 42). Tillich relates the trans-personal category to the "thought of 'God above God',", which he finds implied already in the writings of the Church Fathers; see p. 54. Compare the passage from the Pāli canon: "Since a Tathagata, even when actually present, is incomprehensible, it is enept to say of him—of the Uttermost Person, the Supernal Person, the Attainer of the Supernal—that after dying the Tathagata is, or is not, or both is and is not, or neither is nor is not." Samyutta-nikāya III, 118, cited in Conze et al., eds, *Buddhist Texts through the Ages,* p. 106.

54   Abe, "Buddhism and Christianity as a Problem of Today," p. 24.

55   Buddhadāsa, *Dhamma—The World's Saviour,* p. 34.

56   Nishitani, "The Personal and the Impersonal in Religion," pp. 82-88.

57   Abe, "Buddhism and Christianity as a Problem of Today," p. 29.

58   J. B. Lotz, "Personalismus I," *Lexikon für Theologie und Kirche,* vol. VIII (Freiburg, 1963), p. 293. Similarly Lotz writes that "Being. in things is alienated from itself . . . it attains or possesses itself only in the person. Therefore things are manifest as a lesser being, excelled by the person as a being in the full sense of the word. Being is intrinsically personal, and for this reason it defines its self fully only as person." Lotz, "Sein," *Handbuch theologischer Grundbegriffe* II (Munich, 1963), p. 540. In this view, being finds its fullest expression in the human and, preeminently though analogically, in the Divine Person. Yet even the material lesser being of things reflects the personal in some degree. Thus this view might be used as a philosophic approach to Teilhard's conception of a personalized universe.

59   H. Mühlen's interpretation of the general experience of being as a Thou-experience concludes that "Existence means existing as a Thou" ["*Da-sein ist Du-sein.*"]. By applying the personalistic method, he attempts to show that "the inner dynamic of personal behavior . . . transcends every limitation, even the restriction of other persons, towards the unlimited Thou." See "Das unbegrenzte Du: Auf dem Wege zu einer Personologie," in *Wahrheit und Verkündigung: Festschrift Michael Schmaus* (Munich-Paderborn-Wien, 1967), pp. 1259-1285, quotations from pp. 1285, 1283. Compare the impressive report of a personal Thou-experience by the French founder of the "medicine of the person," Paul Tournier, "Der unsichtbare Dritte," *Transzendenz als Erfahrung; Festschrift Graf Dürckheim* (Weilheim, 1966), pp. 343-346.

60   J. B. Lotz, "Auf dem Wege zum personalen Transzendenten," *Festschrift Graf Dürckheim,* pp. 237-250, esp. 243-245.

61   There is, however, report of a creation myth (in the broad sense of the term) in later Buddhism which extensively describes the origin of the world but names no creative power. Cf. the quotation from Agganna Suttanta, Digha Nikāya XXVIII in

Hajime Nakamura, "Die Grundlehren des Buddhismus. Ihre Wurzeln in Geschichte und Tradition," *Buddhismus der Gegenwart,* p. 25.

62   Buddhadāsa, *Christianity and Buddhism,* p. 80.

63   *Ibid.,* pp. 81-93.

64   *Ibid.,* p. 83.

65   *Ibid.,* p. 83.

66   D. J. Ehr, "Creation, Theology of," *New Catholic Encyclopedia* IV (New York, 1967), p. 423.

67   Joseph Ratzinger, "Schöpfung," *Lexikon für Theologie und Kirche* IX (Freiburg, 1964), p. 461.

68   *Ibid.,* p. 460.

69   The expression *"creatio ex nihilo"* first appears in the Scriptures in 2 Macc. VII, 28, a relatively late passage in the Old Testament.

70   Abe, "Buddhism and Christianity as a Problem of Today," p. 12. Cf. the extensive discussion of the phrase *"creatio ex nihilo,"* pp. 10-21.

71   Ratzinger, "Schöpfung," p. 461.

72   Michael Schmaus, "Sachhafte oder personhafte Struktur der Welt?," *Interpretation der Welt: Festschrift Romano Guardini* (Würzburg, 1965), p. 695. Schmaus discusses Teilhard de Chardin's thesis of a personalizing universe; he finds truth in this thesis, but also reports his reservations.

73   *Ibid.,* p. 698.

74   *Ibid.,* p. 696.

75   Karl Rahner, "Schöpfungslehre," *Lexikon für Theologie und Kirche* IX (Freiburg, 1964), p. 472.

76   Abe, "Buddhism and Christianity as a Problem of Today," p. 10.

77   *Ibid.,* p. 21.

78   Nishitani, "The Personal and the Impersonal in Religion," p. 14.

79   *Ibid.,* p. 15.

80   *Ibid.,* p. 15.

81   Terms used by Zinzendorf, Hamann, and Bezzel. Compare G. Gloege, "Schöpfung IV B. Dogmatisch," *Religion in Geschichte und Gegenwart* V (Tübingen, 1961), p. 1485. Noteworthy in this respect is the work of the Japanese Protestant theologian, K. Kitamori: *Theology of the Pain of God.* According to Kitamori, the pain of God is brought about by the fact that God loves even those who are unworthy of his love—namely those who sin—and sacrifices his beloved son to suffering. P. Nemeshegyi, in an extensive review of Kitamori's book, stresses that the biblical descriptions of the living God do not constitute merely "a symbolic mode of expression which should be retranslated into metaphysical categories"; rather, they are a divine paradox which should stand as it is. "We should therefore let all the biblical *and* metaphysical qualifications of God stand as they are; they are God-given pointers to his unfathomable mystery, in which things which are opposite in our finite universe coincide. Man has to speak about God as suffering *and* rejoicing, unchangeable *and* repenting, acting *and* resting: He is darkness more a-light than light." Cf. review article, *The Japan Missionary Bulletin,* vol. XXI (1967), p. 188.

EPILOGUE

"Homo religiosus on his way" . . .

Our manner of speaking is already symbolic; it captures
our theme in symbols which, though varying from culture to culture, religion to religion, though overlapping
and intermingling, still signify something universally
present. In the East and West alike man is a pilgrim on
his way. This same journey is also symbolized in another widespread form: the passage from one shore to
another. Religious endeavor builds the bridge from this
shore to the shore beyond; a raft carries one across the
waters. The numerous bridges in Japanese Zen gardens

invariably intimate a metaphysical, religious reality; they speak symbolically and signify the passage to the beyond.

Western man understands the symbolic language of the East. The Christian is familiar with the symbols of the bridge and the shore beyond, for he conceives of his own life as a crossing-over.

It is possible to view man's religious way only from the standpoint of the shore on this side. No matter how hard we try, we cannot here know what it is to stand on the shore beyond. Yet the view and the knowledge of life offered by this shore seem to satisfy religious man's need for security. In a shaken world only religion can still grant man this shelter. Even in our present technological age, which apparently seeks to limit man to the things of this world, religion grants man this shelter. It is noteworthy that in spite of the prevalent worldliness of our time, religious demand is stronger than ever. A religious exigence motivates many of today's peoples alienated from traditional religious organizations to grope for surrogates for those shelters.

The Buddhist derives a kind of security from the symbolic knowledge of the two shores. Through practice of his religion and especially in meditation, he attains a certainty of the ineffable. The Christian achieves a secure conviction from his belief in God's Word. Through faith he has access to an undeniable truth of the highest value. Buddhist and Christian will find shelter in different ways and derive security from differing traditional sources; but both will live them out all the more as they go forth in their religious practice believing, trusting, invoking, meditating.

Through the symbols of this shore and the shore beyond, of the passage across on the narrow raft, and of the crossing-over on the swaying bridge, Buddhists and Christians alike experience the paradox of that strength-in-weakness which characterizes the existential situation of religious man and which is of primary importance for the interreligious encounter. On the one hand, religious man derives an incomparable, triumphant, world-overcoming strength from his religious conviction. Is "conqueror" not a title of the Buddha,[1] and does not the New Testament testify to faith as the "victory which overcomes the world"?[2] And yet religious man knows that he has strength in weakness. The Sermon on the Mount—perhaps the only Christian teaching that has fully been accepted by the religious East and, we might say, by all religious people— propounds an ideal of kindness and non-violence which signifies the consummation of man. This is the ideal of strength throughout all the political perils, spiritual revolutions and world catastrophes of the times.

This universally affirmed religious behavior based on strength in weakness is of particular significance for the interreligious dialogue when we come to appraise genuine tolerance. The Christian bases his strength on the conviction that what he holds is true. It is not easy to clarify to the Easterner what truth means to his Western brother, insofar as the Westerner is rooted in Western tradition and embraces the Christian faith with his whole heart. The Christian cannot abandon his belief that the truth which God is, and which God imparts to man, is an Absolute. But when the Christian has understood that strength is contained in weakness, he knows that as a human being he possesses the truth in a human way. He knows that his way of knowing the truth is imperfect and, moreover, that he is not the sole possessor of truth, but that others hold truth as well.

For the truth of the divine *Logos* is spread throughout the world in many and varied forms.

Let us return to the symbolism of the passage between the two shores, and consider one last point. Under this symbolism lies an abysmal loneliness, the loneliness of human existence which Pascal referred to when he said "*On meurt seul*," and which the Japanese Zen master and artist Hakuin expressed in his many versions of the "Blind Men Crossing a Bridge."[3] In East and West, this loneliness has been profoundly experienced by religious man. But it cannot serve as the last word on man's religious experience. Man is not alone on his passage between the two shores. For he also experiences a solidarity with all men, especially today among the growing awareness of the unity of the human race on earth. Thus love and compassion with all, from which spring joy and peace, are the words for the fullness of religious experience. We are finding solidarity on the way through encounter and dialogue; a relationship is growing, and already fruit has been borne.

The dialogue between Buddhists and Christians not only invites us to reflect on the past, on history, but also offers an opportunity for turning to the future. It is one of the unique marks of our times that the religions are more than ever aware of their responsibility for man's future, and not simply of their need to adapt to the tasks of the times by modernizing themselves. And at the same time, it seems that in accentuating the new and the future, the religions have a unique contribution to make—because they spring from the roots of reality and aim for ultimate reality. The interreligious dialogue bears in its part the future of mankind. A new horizon is opening up, and dialogue is perhaps one of mankind's greatest hopes.

Notes

1   *Jina:* the victor, the conqueror, is one of the titles given to the Buddha in the Pāli canon. A life of Shākyamuni appeared in Ceylon in the 13th century under the title *Jinacarita;* see E. J. Thomas, *The Life of Buddha as Legend and History* (London, 1949), pp. 50, 282. The expression *"jinasya sāsanam"* is used as a synonym for the teachings of the Buddha; see S. Mochizuki, *Bukkyō Daijiten,* vol. V (Tokyo 1958), p. 4441.

2   1 John. V, 4.

3   Cf. print no. 82 in Yasuichi Awakawa, *Zen Painting* (Tokyo, 1970); also the prints no. 54a, 54b, and 55 in K. Brasch, *Zenga* (Tokyo, 1961).

INDEX